Jane Roach has produced a classic Bible study on the true meaning of the cross of Jesus Christ. Her stimulating study questions,
insightful commentary, and use of the powerful poetry of classic
hymns of the faith along with her very meaningful and Christ-
exalting prayers will serve as a great resource for individuals and
Bible study groups seeking to dig deeper into the meaning of
the sacrifice made on the cross of Christ. I am happy to endorse
and recommend *Joy beyond Agony*.

> —**J. Carl Laney,** Professor of Biblical Literature, Coor-
> dinator for Israel Study Programs, Western Seminary,
> Portland, Oregon

Joy beyond Agony is an excellent resource that puts the biblical
truth of what Christ has accomplished for Christians on bold
display. True to the Scripture and challenging in every degree,
Jane Roach's approach is accurate in content and elegant in
design. You'll surely benefit from the thoughtful questions
and the opportunity to reflect on what the suffering Savior
did for us.

> —**Allen R. Taha,** Pastor, Trinity Presbyterian Church (PCA),
> Boerne, Texas

Jane Roach's book on Jesus' crucifixion and cross takes us to the
very center of our faith. Roach reminds us that the cross, which
was a scandal in Paul's day, is still scandalous today. At the same
time, we see that the cross is our only hope and our greatest joy.
In the cross we find both the provision for our sin and the pattern
for our lives. Roach's work is biblically rooted and devotionally

powerful. Readers will be encouraged and challenged by this wonderful treatment of the cross.

—**Thomas Schreiner,** James Buchanan Harrison Professor of New Testament Interpretation (1997), Associate Dean of Scripture and Interpretation, Southern Baptist Theological Seminary, Louisville, Kentucky

I highly recommend this Bible study by Jane Roach. It is thorough, doctrinally sound, and speaks to the subject that is central in Christianity but often ignored in churches and Christian publications today—the Cross of Jesus Christ. Jane Roach has taught the Bible for many years and she has taught well. This book is no exception and I see it best used in group Bible study although it could certainly be helpful as a personal daily devotional.

—**Rosemary Jensen,** Founder and President, Rafiki Foundation; former Executive Director, Bible Study Fellowship International

A wonderful tool to introduce the inquirer to the most important person who has stood in human history, who through his life and death brought life out of death and hope for our world. I commend this study tool to any and all readers. It is well written, pedagogically sound, theologically insightful, practically relevant, and personally penetrating. What a useful tool for personal and group Bible study.

—**John Hannah,** Department Chair and Research Professor of Theological Studies, Distinguished Professor of Historical Theology, Dallas Theological Seminary; Adjunct Professor, Redeemer Seminary, Dallas

Joy beyond Agony

Joy beyond Agony

EMBRACING THE CROSS OF CHRIST

Jane Roach

PUBLISHING
P.O. BOX 817 • PHILLIPSBURG • NEW JERSEY 08865-0817

Unless otherwise indicated, Scripture quotations are from the ESV® Bible (The Holy Bible, English Standard Version®), copyright © 2001 by Crossway, a publishing ministry of Good News Publishers. Used by permission. All rights reserved.

Scripture quotations marked (KJV) are from the King James Version.

Italics within Scripture quotations indicate emphasis added.

ISBN: 978-1-62995-095-2 (pbk)
ISBN: 978-1-62995-096-9 (ePub)
ISBN: 978-1-62995-097-6 (Mobi)

Printed in the United States of America

To my friend and mentor, Rosemary M. Jensen, who taught and showed me the importance of the cross of Christ and who opened doors for me to know my Lord and serve him.

Contents

Foreword

THE CROSS HAS ALWAYS been an offense and a scandal to the world, but Christians grasp that it is their only hope. The Jews expected that when the Messiah came he would destroy the Romans and make the Jews the leaders of the world, and then the world would be at peace. On the other hand, the Greeks were convinced that intellectuals would explain the meaning of life. Once the perfect philosophy was formulated, the masses could live according to the wisdom of philosophers.

Christians proclaimed that the world would be transformed only through a man who was crucified. Do you see how bizarre that must have sounded to people two thousand years ago? We are used to the message of Christ crucified because of Christian tradition. But imagine that you had never heard of the cross before. Imagine if someone said today for the first time, "A man who was executed by the political authorities in a small Middle Eastern country is the savior of the world." People instead expect that if God were going to reveal himself to the world, he would do so with power, so that his presence would be unmistakable. His victory over the world would be dramatic, decisive, and easy, and everyone would fear his great power.

Scripture teaches that God chose to bring salvation through a Galilean peasant who was crucified during the Passover feast, and God quietly raised him from the dead (not in the sight of the whole world) three days later. In the second century a Jew by the name of Trypho had a debate with Christian apologist Justin Martyr; Trypho said to Justin during the debate, "Prove to us that he [the Messiah] had to be crucified and had to die such a shameful and dishonorable death, cursed by the law. We could not even consider such a thing" (*Dialogue with Trypho* 90.1).

The Greeks expected a saving message to be intellectually deep and accessible only to the clearest and most profound thinkers. The wise would hear such a message and say, "This is what we intellectuals have always been seeking. This is brilliant." But early Christians proclaimed, "God has chosen to save his people through a man whom he has crucified and raised from the dead."

In this wonderful book, Jane Roach reminds us of the centrality of the cross. Here we have a biblically faithful exposition of what God accomplished in Christ on the cross. But the book isn't only biblically faithful; it is also devotionally rich, for Roach draws us into worship, meditation, and application. Behold the man who was crucified and risen, and be changed forever.

Thomas R. Schreiner

Preface:
The Greatest Gift

WHAT KIND OF GIFT is most precious to you? I am moved by gifts that involve love and sacrifice of time, effort, or money. A gift that costs the giver something expresses immeasurable love. A member of my church, Bette Brasher, is alive today because her husband gave her one of his kidneys. But sacrifices are not limited to life-and-death situations. Perhaps someone missed an important celebration to sit with you while you were ill or to bring you a meal. My brother-in-law built me a wooden nativity set to match the one he made for my sister's grave.

The greatest gift of all is the Lord Jesus Christ, the unique Son of God, becoming our Savior from the penalty, power, and ultimately the presence of sin. I learned about this gift as a child. My church concentrated on the cross of Christ as preparation for celebrating Easter. Each year I anticipated reading of Jesus' passion, which would help me to remember his death and celebrate his resurrection.

As I progressively understood it more deeply, the celebration of his death and resurrection, whether on Resurrection Sunday or through participation in the Lord's Supper, became increasingly personal and glorious. Yet the familiarity of the narrative led me to gloss over it without much thought. I needed a fresh look at the truth of the cross of Christ and the Christ on the cross.

As I looked deeply into my Savior's death, I wanted to give this message to others who need the peace and hope it provided me.

Sadly, there is a growing trend in the church today. The cross of Christ is forgotten in lieu of celebration. However, without the cross, there is no cause for celebration; we are still dead in our sins (John 1:29; 3:16; 8:24). Ignoring the cross robs the celebration of Christ's resurrection of its true meaning—God's affirmation that his servant finished his work of redemption (Isaiah 52:13–53:12). Digging deeply into the events and significance of Christ's cross can be simultaneously challenging and comforting. May you embark on this journey for the joy of growing in the knowledge and love of our Savior.

Acknowledgments

GOD GAVE ME a love for the cross as a child and deepened my understanding of it over the past forty years. My husband, Jim, and my pastor, Dr. Allen Taha, have prayed for me, encouraged me, and believed that God wanted me and would enable me to write this book. Bible Study Fellowship provided invaluable instruction and life application of the cross. Shirley Mills, my BSF coworker, told me ten years ago to write about the cross and faithfully kept the idea before me. Carla Northington, a longtime friend, provided her home for me to teach this study. BSF teaching leader and writer Ava Pennington provided invaluable coaching for publishing. My kind friends Debra Butts, Karen Smith, and Gloria Gartland read and reread the manuscript, offering valuable ideas and corrections. God providentially caused my path to cross with friends whose stories are included. I am grateful for their willingness to include their experiences of enduring pain and agony for the joy of following our Savior. The women attending the Bible studies at Cordillera Ranch in Boerne, Texas, and at my church, Trinity Presbyterian in Boerne, diligently studied the cross, discussed their discoveries, submitted to God's life-transforming applications, and faithfully prayed for me. They taught me as I watched them embrace the cross. Tracy Taha, Chad Swanson, and Pat Macfarlane were kind to help with author photos and videos. Thank you, Amanda Martin and Aaron Gottier from P&R, for your timely help, instruction, and encouragement. To God be the glory for faithfully leading me each step of the way.

Introduction: Digging Deeply

AS YOU BEGIN this Bible study, it is helpful to set spiritual goals—daily Bible study, focused prayer, growth in knowledge, love, patience, and so on. What are your expectations for your spiritual growth and your use of your time? Write them down and refer to them daily, asking God to help you attain them.

Lurking behind our goals and best efforts are our past failures in keeping up with them. These are the kinds of things that agonize us in our Christian life.

- We face the continuing struggle to love the unlovely people in our lives. Remembering how you have experienced God's love when you have been unlovely is a motivation to persevere with others.
- We groan over the lack of self-discipline in daily Bible study and prayer. Scheduling a regular short time each day will have a higher yield over time than trying to do too much. The questions in each chapter will help you begin.
- We start our prayer list without addressing the one eternal God with praise and adoration. Our prayers focus on our felt needs rather than on our spiritual growth and the eternal good of others. Write a few short sentences

that express appreciation for one attribute of God (who he is) and one act of God (what he has done through Christ). You can begin a new habit of prayer by speaking them aloud to God before presenting your needs to him. Remember to include the needs of others, perhaps presenting them to God before your own needs.

- We find ourselves captive to empty pursuits that gobble up precious time we could have used to read, pray, write a note, make a phone call, serve God, or help others. Identify your empty pursuits and begin to replace them one by one with something that honors God and helps others.

- We go to church expecting others to meet our needs while being oblivious to the body language and facial expressions that shout out the pain of another. We ignore the call for help with the activities of our church, begging for a later time that is more convenient. I have never found that God called me to something convenient. God calls us to die to ourselves in order to give life to others. He calls us before we think we are ready so that we will depend on him. The next time you attend church, ask God to open your eyes to see or hear about the needs of others. Trust him to help you reach out to them.

- The guilt of secret sins and the fear of discovery or rejection may hang over us. Jesus died so that we do not have to live with guilt and fear. Admitting your guilt and fear to God is the first step toward freedom from them.

- We may suppress the truth of our sin and think we are basically good. Yet we know the agony of wounding the spirit of another with unkind words, looks, or actions. We disrupt relationships that take a long time to restore.

We hurt others by ignoring them. Confession of sin is a gift from God that provides assurance of forgiveness and cleansing (1 John 1:9).

No matter how shameful your past, how dreadful your present, or how hopeless your future seems, there is a way to break out of the frustration of life as you know it and to live with joy and eternal purpose. Jesus said, "I came that they may have life and have it abundantly" (John 10:10). Jesus endured the agony of his earthly life and cross by anticipating the joy of his completed work through his death, resurrection, ascension, and exaltation (Hebrews 12:1–2). We are called to follow Jesus' example of running with endurance the race God sets before us. Although the pain and sorrow that are part of our race cannot compare to his agony, we, like Jesus, must run with our eyes fixed on the finish line. We press on, anticipating the surpassing joy of the abundant life in his kingdom today and our glorification forever.

Each lesson focuses on some aspect of Jesus' cross that reveals the joy beyond the agony he endured for us. We will consider the gospel accounts along with Old Testament prophecies and promises and New Testament explanations and applications. Each lesson uses beautiful poetry expressed by gifted hymn writers to help us understand the cross. You can hear the tunes at www.cyberhymnal.org or YouTube.

When you read the words of "O Teach Me What It Meaneth" (Lesson 1), you understand that Lucy Bennett knew something of who Jesus was and what he did for her. She longed to know more. She wanted to plumb the depths of his person and work on the cross. Study the suggested hymn as you answer the questions. Put the ancient poetry into prose and vocabulary you can better understand. When you study Shakespeare, you read the language of his day. The same is true for hymn writers of the past who provide a great foundation on which to build. A friend recently told me that she appreciated the hymns when she began to study the Bible. She found herself exclaiming, "That's in the Bible!"

May your study of Christ's life in the Scripture and hymns help you to grow in your knowledge of him and his exceedingly great love for you. "O Teach Me What It Meaneth" might be your prayer as you begin each lesson and answer the questions for personal study and discussion. Writing your insights in the space provided below each question will cement them in your mind and heart. You will find deeper blessing if you complete your personal Bible study before reading the accompanying commentary. It is God's Word, not mine, that gives life!

The Bible has many declarations about believers in relation to the cross of Christ. (When the New Testament uses "I" [or "we"] as an object of God's redeeming love, it means one who believes, not every human being.) John wrote,

> In this the love of God was made manifest among us, that God sent his only Son into the world, so that we might live through him. In this is love, not that we have loved God but that he loved us and sent his Son to be the propitiation for our sins. (1 John 4:9–10)

Paul declared, "I have been crucified with Christ. It is no longer I who live, but Christ who lives in me. And the life I now live in the flesh I live by faith in the Son of God, who loved me and gave himself for me" (Galatians 2:20). The truth is that Christ lives in me. My obligation is that I no longer live by my own strength; I live by faith in the Son of God.[1] As you embrace Jesus' cross by faith, you will begin to understand the joy that is set before you now and forever. Believers in Christ are assured of his presence now and confident that we will be glorified with him in eternity. This hope provides purpose, strength, and comfort for the agony of sorrow and suffering we may encounter.

1. See Steve Green, "Embrace the Cross," on *A Journey of Faith: Steve Green Live in Concert*, Steve Green Ministries, Inc., 2012, compact disc.

Overview: Joy beyond the Agony of the Cross

Let us run with endurance the race that is set before us, looking to Jesus, the founder and perfecter of our faith, who for the joy that was set before him endured the cross, despising the shame, and is seated at the right hand of the throne of God. (Hebrews 12:1–2)

Truth

Jesus endured the cross for the joy set before him, calling and empowering us to follow him.

Hymn: "O Teach Me What It Meaneth"

O teach me what it meaneth
That Cross uplifted high,
With Thee the Man of Sorrows,
Condemned to bleed and die.
O teach me what it meaneth,

That sacred crimson tide,
The blood and water flowing
From Thine own wounded side.

O teach me what it meaneth
For I am full of sin;
And grace alone can reach me,
And love alone can win.
Teach me that if none other
Had sinned, but I alone,
Yet still Thy blood, Lord Jesus,
Thine only must atone.

O teach me what it meaneth,
Thy love beyond compare,
The love that reacheth deeper
Than depths of self-despair.
Yes, teach me, till there gloweth
In this cold heart of mine,
Some feeble, pale reflection
Of that pure love of Thine.

O infinite Redeemer!
I bring no other plea;
Because Thou dost invite me
I cast myself on Thee;
Because Thou dost accept me
I love and I adore;
Because Thy love constraineth,
I'll praise Thee evermore.

—Lucy Ann Bennett, 1908

Opening Prayer

Lord Jesus Christ, we bow before you as the only Savior from sin and the Lord of life. Teach us what it means to live by faith in you, the Son of God. Teach us how to embrace your cross so that we may also begin to understand the joy that awaits your followers in this life and for all eternity. We approach the subject of your sacrificial death in our place and on our behalf with gratitude and with the desire to understand it. While the narrative of the cross may be very familiar, we realize there is much we have not considered about it and we have much to learn. Teach us what it means so that we may worship you more rightly and be changed by the understanding you will give us. May our love for you increase as we realize the extent of your love demonstrated in the cross. For your glory. Amen.

Background

Who was, or is, Jesus? Throughout history his name has inspired hope, compassion, and, in some cases, horrendous acts in the misuse of his name. People today use his name to worship God but also to curse God and others. God declared that the name *Jesus of Nazareth* is above all other names and that every knee in heaven, on earth, and under the earth will one day bow at the mention of it (Philippians 2:9–11).

Many books claim to reveal Jesus. However, the Bible is the chief revelation of Jesus' person, life, and ministry. Jesus was a Jew descended from Abraham and David. He lived two thousand years ago in the region of present-day Israel. The Bible records the following facts about Jesus:

23

- his miraculous birth to a young virgin by the power of the Holy Spirit
- his sinless life that demonstrated his perfect obedience to God the Father
- his announcement of the coming of God's kingdom, which would usher in a new relationship with him as King
- his public ministry of preaching and teaching about the kingdom of God
- his claims to be the Son of God, who was equal with God the Father
- his miraculous signs authenticating his claims to deity
- his conflict with the hypocritical religious leaders who feared losing their power
- his brutal, unjust crucifixion, death, and burial
- his bodily resurrection from the grave three days after his death
- his ascension to the right hand of God, where he reigns in glory
- his coronation as reigning King
- his role as High Priest who prays for his people
- his future return as Judge and King to initiate the new heaven and earth

Jesus' message is called the gospel, or "good news." Through belief in his death in our place and on our behalf, we have our sins forgiven and are reconciled to God. When we are united with him in his resurrection, God gives us a new life so we can live for him. The details of Jesus' death on the cross will help us know how to respond to his claims and work.

It is impossible to consider Jesus' life, message, and claims without responding to them. Was Jesus truly the Son of God? If not, then C. S. Lewis said he was a liar or madman.[1] However, if Jesus' claims are true, then to ignore him is the epitome of folly. Christianity proclaims that Jesus is exactly who he claimed to be. Because he is the Son of God and the only Savior from sin, we can be assured of forgiveness of past sin and guilt, power over sin in the present, and hope for the future removal of the presence of sin.

Questions for Reflection and Discussion

1. What new thoughts about Jesus did you learn from the background section?

---

1. See C. S. Lewis, *Mere Christianity* (1952; repr. New York: HarperCollins, 2001), 52.

2. What response do Jesus' life and claims demand today? What do they demand of you?

3. What do you hope to gain from this study? The hymn "O Teach Me What It Meaneth" may generate some thoughts for you.

Commentary

The world today is into "brands" or visual identities. Individuals, organizations, and businesses spend time, effort, and money creating a logo and mission statement to communicate their values and practices. A brand should be simple and distinctive. What is the "brand" of Christianity? What sets Christianity apart from other world religions or religious beliefs?

When you see the cross, you do not think of Hinduism, Islam, Buddhism, or any other religion. You think Christ, Christian, and Christianity. Paul said it clearly:

> For Christ did not send me to baptize but to preach the gospel, and not with words of eloquent wisdom, lest the cross of Christ be emptied of its power. For the word of the cross is folly to those who are perishing, but to us who are being saved it is the power of God. . . . We preach Christ crucified . . . Christ the power of God and the wisdom of God. (1 Corinthians 1:17–18, 23–24)

The cross is the central message of Christianity. Without it, there is no resurrection, ascension, Pentecost, or eternal life.

To be branded with Christ's cross is not to wear a gold or silver cross around your neck, on your ears, or in your lapel. Those are only reminders of the brand. To be branded with the cross means to embrace and live by what the Bible says about the death of Christ on the cross and what it means for you.

The cross was no accident. Jesus was no victim. His cross was planned before the foundation of the world. It was his set purpose for coming to earth as a man. He came to die. Listen to what the Bible says about his commitment to the cross:

When the days drew near for him to be taken up, he set his face to go to Jerusalem. (Luke 9:51)

Why would he do that?

And taking the twelve, he said to them, "See, we are going up to Jerusalem, and everything that is written about the Son of Man by the prophets will be accomplished. For he will be delivered over to the Gentiles and will be mocked and shamefully treated and spit upon. And after flogging him, they will kill him, and on the third day he will rise." (Luke 18:31–33)

Jesus spoke these words before the cross. Jesus knew all the things written about him. He knew the Old Testament. Knowing what lay ahead, he set his face, determined to go to Jerusalem. Why would he do that?

No one takes [my life] from me, but I lay it down of my own accord. I have authority to lay it down, and I have authority to take it up again. This charge I have received from my Father. (John 10:18)

This is not suicide. Jesus alone had such God-given authority over his death and resurrection. No one else can truthfully make this claim.

Jesus also told us what it meant to follow his example of living in light of God's eternal purpose:

Then Jesus told his disciples, "If anyone would come after me, let him deny himself and take up his cross and follow me. For whoever would save his life will lose it, but whoever loses his

28

life for my sake will find it. For what will it profit a man if he gains the whole world and forfeits his soul? Or what shall a man give in return for his soul? For the Son of Man is going to come with his angels in the glory of his Father, and then he will repay each person according to what he has done." (Matthew 16:24–27)

He did not aim to have a great job, make a name for himself, earn a lot of money, or change the world by worldly methods. He would claim his kingdom by dying on a cross.

The Christian life is a paradox. We have to die to have life, give up to win, lose everything to save it, suffer to gain glory, experience sorrow to have joy. Were you raised to think like that? This is totally opposite to the way the world thinks or teaches. Sadly, it is also not what some churches teach or some professing Christians believe.

How then are we to live as Christians? The Bible charges us to follow Jesus.

Let us also lay aside every weight, and sin which clings so closely, and let us run with endurance the race that is set before us, looking to Jesus, the founder and perfecter of our faith, who for the joy that was set before him endured the cross, despising the shame, and is seated at the right hand of the throne of God. (Hebrews 12:1–2)

What did Jesus endure on the cross? What does it mean that he despised the shame? We will answer these questions and keep before us the truth that death was not the end for Jesus. He was raised, exalted to the place of highest authority. He returned to the eternal glory with his Father that he had enjoyed in eternity past before he came to earth to be a true man. He endured the pain and suffering of dying in our place, on our behalf, because of the joy that he knew lay ahead.

Jesus took our place when he paid the penalty for our sin on the cross. Jesus' example shows us what it means to take up our cross. How often do you read the accounts of the last week of Jesus' life or hear them preached in your church? Perhaps you could tell the story; but it is possible to be very familiar with it and yet miss its intent. Following Jesus includes a sacrificial life of joy that prepares us to reign in glory with him. He has shown us how that is possible. He endured the agony of the cross because of the joy of being exalted at God's right hand and being reunited with him as he had been in eternity past. He also had joy in anticipating his redeemed people who would spend eternity with him, see him in his glory as God, share his glory, and reign with him.

Unlike Jesus' suffering, some of our agony is the result of our own sin, some the result of the accumulation of sin's consequences down through the ages. Hopefully some pain is the result of our testimony of Christ and the witness of our lives, which others will not like. Jesus is exalted at the right hand of God because he accomplished the work God gave him to do as a man. That work was to come to earth and buy back the people whom God had given him as his own but who were alienated from God by sin. We who believe in Jesus as our Savior are those people. We are the reason he came, and we are the reason he could go back to his Father in victory. He bought us back for God by dying in our place. The hope we have is that we will spend eternity glorified with him and that he is present with us now—by his Spirit, in his Word, and as we gather together.

The hope of glory is the "carrot that dangles before the hungry horse." The Christian focus gives proper perspective to the hills and valleys of life on earth. The joy that awaits us strengthens us for the agony of life.

Before reading further, do you have the assurance from the Bible that you have been reconciled to God by Jesus' death on the cross? If so, what thoughts have stirred your heart to love, worship, and serve God? If not, please ask God to give you such assurance as you proceed with the Scripture, hymns, questions, and commentary in this book.

Closing Prayer

O Lord Jesus Christ, teach me what it means that you were uplifted high on the cross . . . that you, the Lord God Almighty, would be the Man of Sorrows, condemned to bleed and die . . . that your sacred blood had to flow from your side on that cross. Teach me because I am full of sin; only your grace can reach me and only your love can win salvation for me. Teach me that if I were the only one who had sinned, your blood would still have been required to atone for my sin. Help me understand my sin and what was needed to atone for it. Use the cross, your agony on it, and your joy in that agony to help me understand it more fully. Then help me to demonstrate more completely what it means to follow you. In your name, Lord Jesus, the only Savior and Redeemer. Amen. (Based on "O Teach Me What It Meaneth")

The Promise of the Cross

Surely he has borne our griefs and carried our sorrows; yet we esteemed him stricken, smitten by God, and afflicted. (Isaiah 53:4)

Text

Isaiah 52:13–53:12

Truth

The suffering and triumphant servant removed our guilt by his sacrificial atonement.

Hymn: "Stricken, Smitten, and Afflicted"

Stricken, smitten, and afflicted,
See him dying on the tree!
'Tis the Christ by man rejected;
Yes, my soul, 'tis he, 'tis he!

'Tis the long-expected Prophet,
David's son, yet David's Lord;
By his Son God now has spoken:
'Tis the true and faithful Word.

Tell me, ye who hear him groaning,
Was there ever grief like his?
Friends thro' fear his cause disowning,
Foes insulting his distress;
Many hands were raised to wound him,
None would interpose to save;
But the deepest stroke that pierced him
Was the stroke that Justice gave.

Ye who think of sin but lightly
Nor suppose the evil great
Here may view its nature rightly,
Here its guilt may estimate.
Mark the Sacrifice appointed,
See who bears the awful load;
'Tis the Word, the Lord's Anointed,
Son of Man and Son of God.

Here we have a firm foundation,
Here the refuge of the lost;
Christ's the Rock of our salvation,
His the name of which we boast.
Lamb of God, for sinners wounded,
Sacrifice to cancel guilt!
None shall ever be confounded
Who on him their hope have built.

—THOMAS KELLY, 1804

Opening Prayer

Heavenly Father, we are sobered by Isaiah's words. The grief and agony he describes go beyond our ability to comprehend. We approach this with a sober mind and heart and, as much as we are able, with the mind and heart of Jesus, who, for the joy that was set before him, endured the agony. May we remember that Jesus' cross was required for his resurrection, ascension, and exaltation to your right hand. Open our eyes to see ourselves, his redeemed people who will join him in heaven, as part of the joy that was set before him.

Teach us by your Holy Spirit to embrace the cross as a demonstration of your holiness and justice, which made the cross necessary, but also of your unsearchable, magnificent love expressed in such an incredible way. May our study give us new depth of understanding of our value to you, our God, and of your willingness to pay the price to redeem us. Teach us, we pray. Amen.

Questions for Study and Discussion

The Lord's Servant

▶ READ ISAIAH 52:13–53:12

1. Circle the words "I," "he," and "we." (In this passage, "I" usually refers to the Lord, "he" to the Lord's servant, and "we" to the servant's disciples.)[1]

---

1. Taken from study note on Isaiah 52:13–53:12 in the *ESV* *Study Bible* (The Holy Bible, *English Standard Version*), copyright 2008 by Crossway, a publishing ministry of Good News Publishers.

2. What new thoughts came to mind as you studied these verses?

3. What effect have these thoughts had on your beliefs about Christ and his death?

The Exaltation of the Servant

▶ READ ISAIAH 52:13–15

4. What good news is proclaimed in 52:13?

5. What do you learn about the Lord's servant from the following verses?

   a. Genesis 3:15

   b. Isaiah 50:6

   c. Isaiah 52:14

6. Read Isaiah 6:1–7; John 12:32–33, 38–41; Hebrews 1:3; and Matthew 28:18. How do they help you understand Isaiah's prophecy of the servant's exaltation?

7. What did you find astonishing about the exaltation of one like the servant?

The Rejection of the Servant

▶ READ ISAIAH 53:1–3

8. How do the word pictures in these verses explain the promised servant's life?

9. How does his life compare with yours?

10. Do you find this servant undesirable or unworthy of your esteem? Why or why not?

11. Why would God designate someone like this "my servant"?

The Sacrifice of the Servant

▶ READ ISAIAH 53:4–6

12. Underline the words "our" and "us" in verses 4–6.

13. How did the people misunderstand the reason for his death?

14. Who struck, smote, and afflicted him?

15. How and why did he suffer?

16. How are you like a sheep gone astray? Give specific examples.

17. How do these facts about the servant affect your understanding of Jesus' cross and your part in it?

The Death of the Servant

▶ READ ISAIAH 53:7–9

18. How does your response to suffering compare to the servant's response to oppression and affliction?

19. How did the servant's generation understand what happened to him (verses 8–9)?

20. Why was it necessary for the servant to suffer in this way?

The Victory of the Servant

▶ READ ISAIAH 53:10–12

21. What was the Lord's will for the servant? What was his reward for accomplishing the Lord's will?

22. What brought satisfaction to the servant, and why is that good news to you?

23. Are you satisfied with what he did? Explain.

Thanksgiving for the Servant

▶ READ ISAIAH 52:13–53:12

24. How do these verses help you to understand God's view of sin and how much God values and loves you?

25. Use the words of this passage and "Stricken, Smitten, and Afflicted" to write a prayer of thanksgiving for God's promise of the cross.

Commentary

Why do we need to study the Old Testament? Should we not focus our attention on the Gospels to learn about Jesus? Or perhaps on the rest of the New Testament that explains who Jesus is and what he did? Reading only the New Testament without the Old Testament is like beginning a mystery without reading the first two-thirds of the book. We find ourselves turning back to find details (who, where, when, how, how long, or why) that the author revealed in the earlier, unread chapters.

The Old Testament prophets repeatedly called the people of Israel to return to their God, the one true God, the Holy One of Israel. They had made gods with their hands in their own image rather than bowing to their Creator, the one who had delivered them out of Egypt through miraculous signs (Isaiah 40:18–26). God promised blessings to the obedient and curses to the rebellious. The prophets recapped these themes as they warned of God's righteous judgment if the people refused to turn back to him. They also promised redemption to the remnant who would believe in the coming Messiah first announced in Genesis 3:15. Let us look closely at God's promised servant, the Messiah.

The prophet Isaiah proclaimed that this Redeemer would be Immanuel, "God with us" (7:14) and God's "servant." Isaiah's four "servant songs" described this person and what he would do for his people. He would bring justice to the nations (42:1–4), lead back the despairing people of Israel with salvation available worldwide (49:1–13), and willingly suffer for the guilt of others (50:4–9). The final song (52:13–53:12) identified the servant as the exalted sin-bearer. It answered the questions Isaiah repeatedly raised: How can God's gracious promises come true for guilty people? How can the Holy One of Israel bless sinful people? How can God love us?

This final song promised what God would do to redeem his people for his purposes and glory. It is the heart of God's purpose of redemption. This suffering servant would drink the cup of God's wrath on behalf of and in place of his people. Isaiah was describing Jesus of Nazareth, the suffering and triumphant servant, who removed our guilt by his sacrificial death on the cross and accounted us righteous (justified) by his triumphant resurrection. This song exclaims how precious God's redemption of his elect is to him—enough to cost the life of his Son. It also proclaims God's view of sin and what it takes for him to forgive it—the death of his sinless Son. Can you imagine ever reading about the cross of Christ without going back to Isaiah?

Three important words explain Jesus' death: *vicarious* ("on behalf of"), *substitutionary* ("in place of"), and *atonement* ("a sacrifice made for the sin or guilt of another"). Jesus Christ is our vicarious, substitutionary atonement. Understanding these words is foundational to understanding Jesus' death on the cross and its meaning for your life.

Do you want to know how much God cares about you, how valuable you are to him? Look at what he paid to make you his own. You might begin each day thanking God by saying, "Thank you that I do not have to pay the penalty for my sins because Jesus Christ is my vicarious, substitutionary atonement. He died on my behalf, in my place, to free me from my sin and guilt."

The servant song consists of five stanzas with three verses each. It promised a person who would successfully bear God's wrath in our place. It explained Jesus' sacrificial death on the cross. Like reading the last chapter of the mystery book first, it began with his exaltation and then moved to his life as a human, his sacrifice (what it entailed, why it was necessary, and what it accomplished), and his death and victory. We see the parallelism of his exaltation and victory, his rejection and death, around the central idea of his sacrifice.

> Exaltation—52:13–15
>   Rejection—53:1–3
>   Sacrifice—53:4–6—The heart of the passage
>   Death—53:7–9
> Victory—53:10–12

Exaltation (Isaiah 52:13–15)

Jesus was exalted, high, and lifted up; he was no ordinary person—he was God himself. He acted wisely by successfully carrying out his Father's will (Luke 22:41–42). Jesus was lifted up on the cross as our sin-bearer (Isaiah 6:1–7; John 12:32–33, 38–41). He rose from the dead and was exalted at the right hand of the Father (Hebrews 1:3), where he reigns with all power and authority (Matthew 28:18–20). This means he has authority over your life and has power to enable you to live for God and his purposes.

His exaltation was astonishing in light of his appalling suffering. The people did not expect a suffering Messiah. They expected a strong king who would rescue them from Roman oppression. His appearance was marred beyond human semblance. He had been beaten into an inhuman mass of bloody flesh. Are you repulsed at the thought of his suffering? It is difficult to talk about something so gross. But it is a picture of what our sin required of him.

We can imagine the result of the beatings on his body and pulling out his beard. But we cannot comprehend the effect that becoming sin had on his physical body. The extremity of his suffering showed the extent of his power to cleanse. He, our High Priest, sprinkled his own blood on many nations, like the priests sprinkled blood of animals on the altar. Many, not all, would be silenced in amazement as they heard the good news of this suffering yet exalted servant. John Newton wrote the hymn "Amazing Grace" in response to understanding his wretched, sinful condition and God's good news of salvation in Jesus Christ.

The agony of Jesus' abuse would become the joy of redeeming the very ones who abused him. Who but God would use the undeserved suffering of his own sinless Son to provide redemption for you and me? This suffering Redeemer is worthy of our worship!

Rejection (Isaiah 53:1–3)

We move from the servant's exaltation to his human life of rejection. The believing remnant of Israel ("us") wondered who would believe their testimony of the power ("arm") of the Lord being revealed through this servant. It would make no sense to their way of thinking. Like a "young plant," he had no impressive credentials or résumé. He was a carpenter, not a regal king or military commander. He was "a root out of dry ground"; his land, Israel, was spiritually dry, but he was deeply rooted in his Father. No one thought he would be the Messiah. His outward appearance did not attract them; he had no desirable beauty. He did not fit their idea of a deliverer.

No one can see the majesty of Christ until God opens the eyes of faith (John 4:24–26). The people closest to Jesus missed his identity (John 1:11). Men despised and rejected his love, character, life, and salvation. His own family did not believe in him (John 7:5). They thought he was crazy (Mark 3:21). Throughout his life, the religious leaders and people despised, rejected, and opposed him. Even in the face of his miracles, they did not esteem him as God. They said he was empowered by Satan (Mark 3:22–23).

He was a true man but was without sin. He experienced things that make us sorrowful. He had no home of his own, no earthly comfort (Matthew 8:20). He was grieved over the sick and hurting people, so he healed them (Mark 1:29–34). He wept at the death of Lazarus (John 11:35). He endured the slanderous words of those who hated him and killed him (Matthew 27:41–44).

However, his sorrow was not because of the pain he experienced. He grieved that people were destroying themselves by rejecting him. He chose to be acquainted with grief out of love for sinful people who despised and rejected him. No wonder he is called the Man of Sorrows.

Jesus Christ bore the grief and sorrow caused by our sin. It is not true that your sin has no effect on others. Sin is like a hand grenade splattering shrapnel and blood over all who are near us. One who sexually abuses a child leaves a stream of brokenness throughout the child's family. A harsh tongue decimates others. Have you grieved over your sin and what it cost Jesus and others? He feels your grief and sorrow more deeply than you ever could. He endured them in your place for the joy set before him. How might the Man of Sorrows help you in your present grief and sorrow? Will you ask him to help you?

Sacrifice (Isaiah 53:4–6)

The servant came to be the vicarious, substitutionary, atoning sacrifice. This truth is the heart of the passage. The suffering servant bore the grief and sorrows of sinful people, like you and me. He was innocent (sinless), yet the people mistakenly thought he was stricken and smitten by God and afflicted for his own sin. People today think the same. Unbelief about their own sin and need for salvation outside of themselves blinds their eyes to Jesus' sinless life.

Jesus substituted himself for us on the cross. Notice the repetition of the words "our" and "us." He carried all the ravages of our sin. Carrying the weight of our guilt was crushing. The chastisement of God that we deserve was upon him so that we can have peace with God. His stripes, the marks of chastisement, brought us healing. The full wrath of God was poured out on him in our place and on our behalf.

Like sheep, all of us are self-willed and have gone astray, each turning to his own way. Have you seen sheep wandering? Totally independent, they scatter and wander from the flock into hazardous areas, sometimes to their death. Every path we choose that is not God's way is sin. We want to control our lives. We put ourselves above God, which is idolatry. We look for love in all the wrong places. Every unkind word or thought of ours is a sin that Jesus bore in his body on our behalf. Do you believe this is true about you? If you are to be forgiven of your sin, some person must pay the cost (Hebrews 9:22). The wages of your sin, what you earn by it, is death (Romans 6:23).

Can we work overtime to get something better? No! Is there a way out for us? Yes! In love for his redeemed people, God sent Jesus to receive our wages—death. "For our sake [God] made

[Jesus] to be sin who knew no sin, so that in [Jesus] we might become the righteousness of God" (2 Corinthians 5:21). To bear our iniquity and guilt meant that Jesus had to become sin and die. There was no other way for God to satisfy his just, holy, righteous character.

Are you carrying your iniquity and guilt on yourself as though that would be enough to satisfy God? Someone has to receive the wages of your sin, but it does not have to be you. God laid on Jesus what you deserve. Will you receive that gracious gift through faith?

Death (Isaiah 53:7–9)

What was Jesus' response to God's laying our iniquity on him? He was silent when oppressed and afflicted during legal proceedings that epitomized the worst possible human injustice (John 18:28–19:16). How do you respond when people tell lies about you? Do you retaliate in anger, slander, or self-defense, or do you speak only to God about it? Do you twist history so that you are the innocent one, using your "selective memory" when it comes to your sin?

Jesus was not a helpless victim, as his generation thought and some say today. His suffering showed absolute commitment to his Father's will and deliberate self-control. He consented to bear God's judgment on behalf of sinners who deserved it (Isaiah 50:5–7). The excruciating death by crucifixion, preceded by enormous suffering, was nothing compared to bearing the undeserved wrath of God. He was cut off from life because of our sin. He was buried with the wicked although he "had done no violence and there was no deceit in his mouth."

He was not a martyr who died for a cause or a saint who lived an exemplary though imperfect life. He was the sinless Son of God and Son of Man (the promised Messiah). He died an innocent man who endured the wrath of God to atone for the guilty. Only an innocent, perfect man could atone for guilty sinners. The sacrifice had to be without blemish. Only God himself could step into that place.

Are you loaded with your sin and guilt? If so, take a careful look at Jesus on the cross taking what you deserve. By faith in him, you may be forgiven.

Victory (Isaiah 53:10–12)

The exalted one of Isaiah 52:13 would complete his Father's will. Fortunately, his death and burial were not the end of the story. His death was not a tragedy. Though crushed, the servant was victorious. His death was necessary to accomplish God's great plan of redeeming a people for himself. He would live to see his offspring—those united to him through faith. Out of the anguish of his soul, the servant would see and also be satisfied that his Father's plan was perfect and that he did his Father's will perfectly.

From the depths of sorrow and suffering, he enjoyed the spoils of victory that God gave him. He is today the resurrected, glorified, ascended Lord and crowned King who made many to be accounted righteous (justified). It is the big exchange: our sins on Jesus and his righteousness given to us. That is the good news of the gospel of Jesus Christ. His resurrection was God's affirmation that his sacrifice was complete and acceptable. God has given Jesus authority to rule the entire universe for him (Matthew 28:18). Now he is glorified before his Father, interceding for the ones whose sins he bore (Hebrews 7:25). This was the joy he anticipated as he suffered.

By faith in God's promise, we are there with and in him:

> But God, being rich in mercy, because of the great love with which he loved us, even when we were dead in our trespasses, made us alive together with Christ—by grace you have been saved—and raised us up with him and seated us with him in the heavenly places in Christ Jesus. (Ephesians 2:4–6)

If you believe that Jesus is your substitutionary atonement, you may write your name in these verses. You live on earth, but you are already seated with God in Christ in the heavenly places. You will be like him in his eternal kingdom (1 John 3:2).

Like looking at the forest instead of the trees, we are able to see our lives from a different perspective. God sees our circumstances as preparation for our eternal state. Knowing these truths enabled Jesus to endure the agony of his suffering for us. It enables us to endure life's struggles as well.

The promise of this servant song is that God the Son would become a man rejected by those he came to save. Sinless and perfect, he would be the atoning sacrifice for their sin. This man was Jesus of Nazareth. He would receive the penalty of death that we earned for our sin and would remove the guilt that we experience because of it. He would perfectly fulfill God's just requirements for satisfying his divine wrath against sin. He would fulfill all the Scripture required and prophesied about God's redeeming a people for himself.

He agonized in death as he bore the wrath of God because of our sin. This rightly overwhelms us. He anticipated the joy of his triumph of satisfying the will of his Father and receiving the reward of making many righteous through his suffering. "Many" does not mean all, but only those who receive him through faith as their perfect sin-bearer. Are you one of them?

What does this tell you about God's love for you and the value he places on you? Through faith in the servant, you are accepted and forgiven by the one true and holy God. He wipes away your guilt so that you do not have to carry it. You are accounted righteous because Jesus poured out his soul to death for your transgressions (violations of his law) and sins (deliberate acts of disobedience).

Are you satisfied with what Jesus did? God was satisfied. Jesus was satisfied. Do you still think you can or must do something to save yourself? Pray more, give more, love more, and read the Bible more? You can do nothing except receive Jesus Christ, God's gift to you. This was an enormous price to pay for your redemption.

Would you offer up your beloved child to go through what Jesus did so that someone else could be saved? As you look at Jesus, he says, "Your union with me in glory is worth all the pain, rejection, sorrow, and agony of my life, of my steps to the cross, and of what I endured on the cross. I am satisfied because you are justified through my death and resurrection. Your union with me was the joy I anticipated and kept before me as I went through the agony of the cross. You are that precious to me!"

Will you believe and embrace how much God gave to redeem you? It is not arrogant to say you are loved that much. It is humble to agree with what God has said and demonstrated (Romans 5:8). What else is vying for your "self-worth"—name, home, position, reputation, possessions, power, success of children that makes you look good as a parent, or even service for him? The agony of letting go of these things will seem like nothing compared to the joy of knowing the love of God that was demonstrated in Christ and his cross. He alone can fill your deepest needs and bring you the greatest joy. Finding your satisfaction in Jesus is true joy, the abundant life he came to give (John 10:10).

Caroline abandoned her pride and self-reliance as she clung to Christ's cross and mercy. "Two months after I turned twenty-two, I was diagnosed with colon cancer; two months after that, I was having surgery to remove my entire colon. I had little fear; my confidence in God was strong and he granted me his peace. Much to my surprise, less than a week after my surgery, I was told that the cancer was more aggressive than expected and chemotherapy was highly recommended.

"From the first moment I told others about having cancer, I was flooded with support, particularly from my church communities. These offers were encouraging leading up to the surgery; but the generosity soon became overwhelming as I began to share about the unhappy diagnosis and impending treatment. I had two church communities at my back, despite the fact that I lived far away from one and had only recently joined another. I had friends offering to serve and help me in even unglamorous ways. I had bare acquaintances praying devotedly for me at the request of mutual friends. The more kindness I was shown, the more frustrated I became, and the more frustrated I grew with myself for being so ungrateful.

"When I finally put words to my frustration, I realized I was angry that I was utterly undeserving. I did not deserve the outpouring of support from my friends, but it was my unworthiness and inability to repay that made their gifts truly beautiful. As one who has always struggled with pride, my health struggle has been, and continues to be, a lesson in humility. For if I feel that I am brought to my knees by the love shown me by my friends, on whom the fate of my immortal soul does not depend, how much more must I fall facedown on the ground before the cross? Christ's is the ultimate undeserved gift, and it is one I cannot afford to scorn. I must look to the cross and cling to it. It will not be on my own power that I make it through these times. I must—there is no other way—I must abandon my pride and self-reliance and cling to his cross and his mercy."

What will you do to enjoy being his purchased prize now and joyfully anticipate being with him and like him forever? Turning your thoughts to him and his sacrificial death for you will cause life's circumstances, both pleasant and painful, to pale in comparison with your present position in him and with your future glory in heaven. You can begin by reciting these truths and thanking him daily for them. "Thank you, Lord Jesus Christ, for being the Lamb of God who has taken away my sin."

Closing Prayer

Lord Jesus, you were stricken, smitten, and afflicted when you died on the cross. Men rejected you. No one ever knew grief like yours. Your fearful friends deserted you. Your enemies insulted you. Many were quick to raise their hands to strike you, to hit your head, to pull out your beard, to lash your back. No one came to your aid. The deepest pain was the stroke that the Father laid on you to pay for my sin. Thank you for willingly taking that painful stroke. May I neither think lightly of my sin nor believe that my evil is so great that I cannot be saved from it. Help me to view the nature of sin correctly and to understand the guilt it incurred. You, Christ, are the Rock of my salvation, the name in which I boast, the Lamb of God wounded for me and sacrificed to cancel my guilt. May that be the firm foundation on which I stand, the refuge to which I flee, and the hope I hold out to the lost. I love you, Lord Jesus, and I receive the love that you have demonstrated for me on the cross. For your honor and glory and the furtherance of your kingdom. Amen.

The Person on the Cross

Long ago, at many times and in many ways, God spoke to our fathers by the prophets, but in these last days he has spoken to us by his Son, whom he appointed the heir of all things, through whom also he created the world. He is the radiance of the glory of God and the exact imprint of his nature, and he upholds the universe by the word of his power. After making purification for sins, he sat down at the right hand of the Majesty on high. (Hebrews 1:1–3)

Texts

Selections related to Jesus' person and work, as noted in the questions and commentary.

Truths

Jesus of Nazareth was true God and true man. He claimed to be one with God, and his works authenticated his claims.

Hymn: "Man of Sorrows! What a Name"

Man of Sorrows! what a name
For the Son of God, who came
Ruined sinners to reclaim:
Hallelujah! what a Savior!

Bearing shame and scoffing rude,
In my place condemned he stood,
Sealed my pardon with his blood:
Hallelujah! what a Savior!

Guilty, vile, and helpless, we;
Spotless Lamb of God was he;
Full atonement! can it be?
Hallelujah! what a Savior!

Lifted up was he to die,
"It is finished!" was his cry;
Now in heav'n exalted high:
Hallelujah! what a Savior!

When he comes, our glorious King,
All his ransomed home to bring,
Then anew this song we'll sing:
Hallelujah! what a Savior!

—PHILIP P. BLISS, 1875

Opening Prayer

Man of Sorrows, Son of God, the radiance of the glory of God and the exact imprint of his nature, you came to reclaim us, ruined sinners. You have finished your work and are seated at the right hand of the Majesty on high. From there you uphold the universe by the word of your power. Help us to know more about you and to proclaim now and in the ages to come, "Hallelujah! what a Savior!" Amen.

Questions for Study and Discussion

The person on the cross is Jesus of Nazareth.

1. What facts about the person on the cross do you find in Genesis 1:1; John 1:1–4; Colossians 1:16–20; and Hebrews 1:2–3?

2. How do these facts help you to understand who you are, why you are here, and where you are going?

3. What do you learn, from John 1:14; Philippians 2:3–6; and Hebrews 2:17–18; 4:14–16, about this person's relationship to people?

4. Why is this relationship necessary for Jesus and for you?

5. Summarize your answers to questions 1–4 with one sentence describing Jesus of Nazareth. How do Isaiah 7:10–17 and Matthew 1:23 compare with your summary?

6. Why is it important that Jesus of Nazareth, the person on the cross, is both true God and true man?

7. Read John 20:30–31. What do you learn about Jesus from John's purpose in writing his gospel?

8. State Jesus' claims about himself and explain the metaphors he used.

    a. Matthew 9:6 with Daniel 7:13–14

    b. John 6:33–35

c. John 8:12

d. John 10:7–11

e. John 11:25–26

f. John 14:6

g. John 15:1

h. John 10:30; 14:9

How have you experienced Jesus in any of these ways?

9. Describe the works of Jesus of Nazareth and what each reveals about him.

   a. John 6:1–14

b. John 6:16–21

c. Matthew 8:1–3

d. Matthew 9:6

e. Matthew 15:30–31

10. How do Jesus' works relate to his claims?

11. What is your response to the claims and works of Jesus? What are the consequences of your response?

12. Explain your understanding of the person on the cross and the work he did there for you. Refer to previous lessons and to "Man of Sorrows! What a Name."

Commentary

Who was Jesus? Who is Jesus? How would you respond to those questions if they were asked by a committed Christian? What would you say to an avowed atheist? How would you explain to a child in Sunday school or to your own child or grandchild? Does it matter? Why?

John quoted Jesus as saying,

> "And I, when I am lifted up from the earth, will draw all people to myself." He said this to show by what kind of death he was going to die. (John 12:32–33)

This was quite a claim to power—"all people to myself." *All* refers to all kinds of people, not to every individual. (The claim that every individual will eventually be saved is universalism.) How did Jesus have such authority? Why can we believe him? Was he some egomaniac? Was he kidding himself and others? These are no small questions. They are crucial to the study of the cross and of its meaning in our lives.

We approach this lesson with the same presuppositions that we bring to all of them: The Bible is the very Word of God. Because God is perfect and cannot lie, so is his Word. It is without error. Thus, we look to it to see what God reveals about Jesus Christ, about us, and about life.

Jesus of Nazareth was a true man; he was also true God. The Bible makes both claims. This is not an easy subject. This truth has been debated throughout the history of the church. We are challenged to think deeply and to cry out to him for understanding. Are his claims trustworthy and life giving? The Bible says they are. Furthermore, his works authenticate his claims.

Let us consider three questions about "the person on the cross."

- What does the Bible say about him?
- What does he say about himself?
- What do you say about him?

As you study Jesus, you may find some of your understanding challenged by what the Bible says. May you come with humility and willingness to see him as he is—two distinct natures in one person. As you ponder his being lifted from the earth on the cross at Calvary, you join those who witnessed this historic event. As you exalt him in your mind and heart, he draws you closer to himself. Only this intimacy can satisfy the deepest longings of your soul.

Perhaps you feel that life is just the way you want it—good health, success, security, comfort. . . . What happens if your portfolio tumbles, your doctor gives a grim diagnosis, or your cherished loved one rebels or rejects you? Knowing the person on the cross provides a way to go through such turmoil with peace and even joy.

What Does the Bible Say about Him?

God, the Creator

The Bible begins by identifying this person as God himself. The first words in the Bible proclaim that God created the heavens and the earth (Genesis 1:1). The apostle John explained that the one by whom and through whom everything was made is "the Word." He is the eternal, preexistent Word, who is uniquely the Son of God and who is himself God (John 1:1–4; Philippians 2:6). He was the sole agent through whom all things were made.

Paul identified this Creator as Jesus of Nazareth, the one by whom and for whom all creation was made (Colossians 1:16). Did you know you were made for Jesus? He made you for his pleasure and glory. You have purpose and meaning beyond yourself. Viewing life from your relationship to him as your Creator may be a paradigm shift for you. How does this change your view of who you are, why you are here, where you are going, and what you are doing?

Jesus holds all things together (Colossians 1:17) and upholds the universe by the word of his power (Hebrews 1:3). Do you see why he had to rise from the dead? If he were in the tomb, how could all things be held together in him? If he stopped holding all things together, the heavens, earth, and all its inhabitants would blow apart into utter chaos. This truth is comforting when your own world seems falling apart, for there is one who holds it together.

Jesus of Nazareth, the Man

The Word willingly became a man—Jesus of Nazareth—and dwelt among men (John 1:14). In taking the form of a man, he experienced the same limitations common to all people. He was hungry, tired, hot, restricted to one place at a time. He did not resort to his deity to turn stones into bread when tempted by Satan or to call down legions of angels at his arrest. He considered himself a servant who counted the interests of others more significant than his own (Philippians 2:3–4, 6). He became one of us (Hebrews 2:17–18) that we might become one with him. Matthew 1:23 presents him as the fulfillment of Isaiah's prophecy of the one to be born, a man, who would be "God with us" (Isaiah 7:14).

The Bible includes two genealogies of Jesus. Matthew (1:1–17) emphasized Jesus' legal claim to the throne of David, qualifying him to be the Messiah (2 Samuel 7:16). He also showed him descended from Abraham, alluding to him as the one through whom all peoples would be blessed (Genesis 12:3). Luke began his genealogy, "Jesus . . . being the son (as was supposed) of Joseph" and ended with "Adam, the son of

God" (Luke 3:23–38). No other biblical genealogy includes the words "the son of God."

Adam, the first man, could rightly be called the son of God. His birth was unique—God formed him and breathed into him the breath of life (Genesis 2:7). All other human births came from Adam—first Eve (fashioned from Adam's rib), then their descendants through the male sperm uniting with the female egg. However, Adam sinned and we are "in" him, so we are included in his fall and are called "sons of Adam."

Jesus, the perfect Son of God, also had a unique birth. He was not conceived by sexual union of a man and woman. He was born of a virgin by the Holy Spirit and the power of the Most High (Luke 1:35). Yet he willingly became part of Adam's imperfect family. This qualified him to redeem them.

> Christ the Son of God
> Became a son of Adam
> That we sons of Adam
> Might become sons of God![1]

Paul explains,

> For as in Adam all die, so also in Christ shall all be made alive. . . . Just as we have borne the image of the man of dust, we shall also bear the image of the man of heaven. (1 Corinthians 15:22, 49)

Jesus of Nazareth is both true God and true man in one person. Yet he was no ordinary man. He was equally true God,

1. R. Kent Hughes, *Luke: That You May Know the Truth*, vol. 1 (Wheaton, IL: Crossway Books, 1998), 129.

the Creator of all things, Son of God, and the Messiah promised in the Old Testament. How does your belief about Jesus of Nazareth compare with the truth that he is both true God and true man in one person? How can you align your beliefs with what the Bible teaches? Why is this important?

What Does Jesus Say about Himself?

The Son of Man

Jesus called himself the "Son of Man" (Matthew 9:6). This was Jesus' favorite title for himself. This was not a statement of his humanity but a claim to be the Messiah prophesied in Daniel 7:13–14. He also claimed he had authority on earth to forgive sins, something only God could do. He validated that claim to deity by healing a paralytic (Mark 2:1–12).

I Am

The apostle John wrote his gospel with a specific goal in mind:

> Now Jesus did many other signs in the presence of the disciples, which are not written in this book; but these are written so that you may believe that Jesus is the Christ, the Son of God, and that by believing you may have life in his name. (John 20:30–31)

John recorded seven statements that Jesus made about himself, each beginning with "I am." God alone could truthfully make such claims. Jesus' words "I am" identified him with God's revelation to Moses at the burning bush. "God said to Moses, 'I AM WHO I AM' . . . Say this to the people of Israel, 'I AM has sent me to you'" (Exodus 3:14).

The Bread of God. After feeding five thousand people with five loaves of bread and two small fish, Jesus claimed to be "the bread of God" who "comes down from heaven and gives life to the world" (John 6:33). This pointed back to God's provision of manna in the wilderness (Exodus 16). He said, "I am the bread of life; whoever comes to me shall not hunger, and whoever believes in me shall never thirst" (John 6:35). Bread satisfies hunger and strengthens the body. More than satisfying our basic need for physical food, Jesus satisfies the longing of our souls. We need to know that our lives are based on what is right and that our relationship with God is not hindered by sin. Even more, he gives us a desire for himself that goes deeper into our souls. On a scale of 1 to 10, how do you rate your desire for Jesus?

Jesus provides strength to live for him rather than for ourselves and to persevere through life's challenges. Where do you need his strength today? Have someone's comments tempted you to doubt the truth of the Bible? Do you need to forgive someone? Do you need to stay away from the latest "toys" until you have paid off your credit card(s)? Are you in a relationship that is luring you into "something beautiful" that God calls sin? You may find instant gratification in disobeying God's will, but it is only temporary. Jesus will provide true, lasting satisfaction and strength to live for God's purposes and glory.

The Light of the World. Jesus said, "I am the light of the world" in the context of the Feast of Tabernacles (John 8:12). This feast included ceremonies symbolizing Israel's desert wanderings after the exodus. His Jewish audience would remember the cloud and pillar of fire in the wilderness, assuring them of God's glorious presence, guidance, and protection. During the feast, the temple was spectacularly illuminated for the entire city to see. In this setting, Jesus stood teaching on the final day of the feast. There he identified himself as the true light of the world.[2] Thus, Jesus claimed to be the manifestation (glory) of God in the exodus. He was present to guide and protect his people.

Jesus guides his people through the dark places that we face in our families, workplaces, and culture. He does not appear as a cloud or fire; he directs us through the Bible.

The Door of the Sheep and the Good Shepherd. Jesus said, "I am the door of the sheep" and "I am the good shepherd" (John 10:7, 11). He is the entrance into the sheepfold that is the kingdom of God. He would lead his sheep in and out of the fold (give them free access) to find God's nourishing provision, depicted by food, water, and rest (Psalm 23). He would also provide protection and care, keeping his sheep in and predators out. He would know his sheep intimately, calling them by name, and they would recognize his voice. How do his sheep recognize his voice? The Bible is the way his voice leads and guides us today.

The Resurrection and the Life. Jesus said, "I am the resurrection and the life. Whoever believes in me, though he die, yet shall he live, and everyone who lives and believes in me shall never die" (John 11:25–26). He is the giver of physical and spiritual life, the source of life now and of the life to come. Eternal life is found only in relationship with Jesus (John 17:3). Death has no power over his people; they need not fear death and dying. He raises his people to union with him, seated with God in him in the heavenly places (Ephesians 2:6).

2. For further information, see the note on John 8:12 in *The Archaeological Study Bible* (Grand Rapids, MI: Zondervan, 2005).

The Way, the Truth, and the Life. Jesus said, "I am the way, and the truth, and the life. No one comes to the Father except through me" (John 14:6). This is the most exclusive statement ever made. He is the only way to God. He removed the barrier of our sin, providing access to God and to his gracious mercy and help (Matthew 27:51; Hebrews 4:16). He is the solution to our alienation from God. It is a blatant lie of our culture that all religions lead to God and let us enter the bliss of his eternal presence. It is true that all will face God. However, only those who come through Jesus will find his loving arms ready to embrace them. Those who reject Jesus will come face to face with him as their holy and righteous Judge; he will declare them guilty and they will be forever under his wrath (Revelation 20:15).

He is not "a" truth but "the" truth—the fulfillment of Old Testament Law and the revelation of the one true God. He defined truth by his person. He told and showed us what to believe and how to live accordingly. He is the life. He has life in himself and is able to give eternal life to those who believe in him (John 3:16; 5:26). Jesus' statement amounted to a claim to deity. "Jesus is the only authorized revelation of God in human form and he is the only authorized representative of humanity to God."[3] How much we need this revelation of Jesus in our age of biblical illiteracy and religious pluralism.

The True Vine. Jesus said, "I am the true vine" (John 15:1). Christians are united with him, and his life flows into us. By his nature, he brings fruit to God the Father and also produces the fruit of his Spirit in his people. This claim was in stark contrast

3. *The Expositor's Bible Commentary*, ed, Frank E. Gaebelein, vol. 9: *John, Acts* (Grand Rapids: Zondervan, 1988), 144.

with Old Testament Israel's failure to produce the fruit God expected (Isaiah 5:1–7).

One with the Father

In addition to these seven "I am" statements, Jesus said, "I and the Father are one" (John 10:30). This was a claim to be equal with God the Father. He stated that to see him was to see the Father (14:9). The author of Hebrews further explained, "He is the radiance of the glory of God and the exact imprint of his nature" (Hebrews 1:3).

What Do You Say about Him?

Jesus was not all talk. He validated his words with his life. His miraculous feeding of five thousand was recorded in all four gospels. He walked on water and calmed a storm by commanding it to be still. He made the lame walk, the blind see, the dumb speak, and the deaf hear (Matthew 11:1–5). These miracles would identify Messiah (Isaiah 26:19; 29:18–19; 35:5). His touch healed those in his presence; his word healed those far away. Lazarus died and was in the tomb three days. When Jesus called, "Lazarus," he walked out of the grave alive. Jesus was transfigured on a mountaintop in front of his disciples. His works were superhuman. No mere human could do what Jesus did. The evidence for his deity is abundant and sufficient. "Now there are also many other things that Jesus did. Were every one of them to be written, I suppose that the world itself could not contain the books that would be written" (John 21:25).

Jesus by his words claimed to be God and by his works demonstrated that he is God. What claims of Jesus are new to you? What does his claim to be God mean for you? Which of the "I am" statements do you need to remember today? Do you need satisfaction and strength, guidance, protection and peace, assurance of life and courage to face death? Do you need discernment and truth? He promises to be the answer to all these needs.

Tom was a hardcore alcoholic and a Marine Corps veteran of Vietnam. "I ridiculed Christians when I was drunk, and when sober I tuned them out. Yet God sought me individually. Although I ran for several years, God's steadfast love brought me to Christ. It was the greatest gift ever. I will never get over the wonder that God loves me so much."

When diagnosed with cancer in 2010, Tom determined that his personal relationship with God, not cancer statistics, was what really mattered. He trusted that God sovereignly gives each of us what we need to glorify him. Yes, even cancer was a gift from God, who knew what was best for Tom. Through much agony, he was strengthened by God to see beyond his treatment and pain to the eternal needs of medical personnel, other patients, and friends. With each hospitalization, he believed his cross was to tell them the gospel, the loving call of his Good Shepherd. His uncomplaining spirit gave credibility to the goodness of his Savior.

Three and a half years later, Tom faced physical death while clinging to the truth of his union with Jesus. He asked to be alert right to the end, to know what was happening around him. "I want my focus to be Christ on the cross. This helps me realize how much more he suffered, including what he suffered for me. I am strengthened by Scripture I memorized, which can never be taken away, even in a hospital." When weak, Tom drew his strength from Jesus. God entrusted Tom with suffering, and Tom glorified him in it by enjoying him and his perfect will. Tom was not all talk. He demonstrated with his life what it means to follow Jesus. Tom anticipated being glorified and seeing Jesus! Tom was confident that death is the way into God's loving embrace.

Encountering Jesus through his words and works demands a response. What is your response to this truth about Jesus of Nazareth, the person on the cross, who is true God and true man? He is not the figment of one's imagination or speculation. He is the revelation of God's holiness and love shouting from the cross, a real event in history.

Will you study diligently to be convinced of these great truths for you and those you love? Ask him to show you how he is each of the "I am" statements for you. You will find joy as you run the race God has for you.

Closing Prayer

Lord Jesus, help me to understand these simple yet profound truths about you. Knowing you in an intimate relationship will help me to understand more deeply what you have done for me. Increase my desire for you as I encounter your words and your works in your Word. Turn my mind and heart to anticipate the day you will come as glorious King to bring home all those you ransomed by your blood. May I shout from the depths of my heart, "Hallelujah! what a Savior!" For your glory. Amen.

The Prayers Leading to the Cross

And now, Father, glorify me in your own presence with the glory that I had with you before the world existed. (John 17:5)

And he withdrew from them about a stone's throw, and knelt down and prayed, saying, "Father, if you are willing, remove this cup from me. Nevertheless, not my will, but yours, be done." And there appeared to him an angel from heaven, strengthening him. And being in an agony he prayed more earnestly; and his sweat became like great drops of blood falling down to the ground. (Luke 22:41–44)

Texts

Matthew 26:36–56
Mark 14:33–50
Luke 22:39–53
John 17:1–18:12

Truth

Prayer includes both joy and agony.

Hymn: "Go to Dark Gethsemane"

Go to dark Gethsemane,
Ye that feel the tempter's power;
Your Redeemer's conflict see,
Watch with Him one bitter hour:
Turn not from His griefs away—
Learn from Jesus Christ to pray.

Follow to the judgment hall,
View the Lord of life arraigned;
O the wormwood and the gall!
O the pangs His soul sustained!
Shun not suffering, shame or loss—
Learn from Him to bear the cross.

Calvary's mournful mountain climb;
There, adoring at His feet,
Mark the miracle of time,
God's own sacrifice complete:
"It is finished!" hear Him cry—
Learn from Jesus Christ to die.

—JAMES MONTGOMERY, 1820

Opening Prayer

Gracious God, our Father, teach us how to pray as our Savior did. May we be honest in expressing both our joy and our sorrow. We will never experience the agony he had on our behalf, but life is full of surprises, some very painful. May we not just "say a prayer," but pray earnestly, as we embrace your will for us. Help us to learn from our Savior how to approach you. Help us also to know when to end our prayers, submit to your will, and rise up to face what lies ahead in your strength and power. For your glory, Amen.

Questions for Study and Discussion

Jesus Prayed for Himself

▶ READ JOHN 17:1–5

1. What did Jesus request from his Father?

2. How had Jesus brought glory to his Father?

3. What work did Jesus come to do? (See lesson 1.)

4. Explain Jesus' statement in verse 3.

Jesus Prayed for His Disciples

▶ READ JOHN 17:6–19

5. Why did Jesus value his disciples?

6. Describe what the disciples might face when Jesus was no longer with them. How did Jesus incorporate these needs into his prayer?

7. For whom might you pray these requests?

Jesus Prayed for All Believers

▶ READ JOHN 17:20–26

8. Was Jesus praying for you? How can you know?

9. How does the truth that Jesus prayed for believers encourage you?

10. What effect does Christian unity or disunity have on the proclamation of the gospel?

11. How can you promote the unity that Jesus described in your family and church?

▶ READ MATTHEW 26:36–46; MARK 14:33–42;
AND LUKE 22:39–46

12. Describe the scene in Gethsemane to someone who has not read the Bible. What questions might they ask you, and how would you answer them?

13. What is "the cup"? (See also Psalm 75:8; Isaiah 51:17; and
    Mark 15:23–24, 34.)

14. What details help you to understand the depths of Jesus' sorrow? How are you helped?

15. Can you have a "Gethsemane" like Jesus had? Why or why not?

▶ READ MATTHEW 26:47–56; MARK 14:43–50;
LUKE 22:47–53; AND JOHN 18:1–12

16. When facing arrest, what did Jesus do that shows his submission to the Father's plan?

17. How do the events in Gethsemane display Jesus' deity?

18. How do Jesus' prayer and action encourage you to seek his help today?

19. Review your answers and "Go to Dark Gethsemane." Write down your thoughts as you ponder that Jesus fully drank *your* cup. Offer these to God as a sacrifice of thanksgiving.

Commentary

What is prayer? According to the Westminster Shorter Catechism, question 98, "Prayer is an offering up of our desires unto God, for things agreeable to his will, in the name of Christ, with confession of our sins, and thankful acknowledgment of his mercies." Throughout his human life, Jesus spent time alone with the Father, seeking wisdom, guidance, strength, and sweet fellowship. As Jesus approached his death, he poured out his heart to his Father, and then submitted to the will of his God.

Jesus, true man, modeled for us the need for prayer alone with the Father. The Gospels record two prayers in the final hours before his arrest. The first was a time of joyful anticipation and petition in the upper room. The second was a time of agony in Gethsemane. His joy in the midst of his agony came through faith in God's promises. How do your prayers compare to Jesus' prayers?

Joy in the Upper Room (John 17)

Jesus recounted his work on earth and his desire to return to his eternal, preincarnate glory. He desired to take with him those whom the Father had given him. Jesus considered his disciples then and now as love gifts from his Father. I often begin my day by saying, "Thank you, Father, for giving me to Jesus," finding joy and comfort in my relationship with him.

Jesus Prayed for Himself (John 17:1–5)

For His Glorification in the Cross (17:1–3)

Jesus addressed God as "Father" and acknowledged, "the hour has come." His arrest, crucifixion, death, and burial were imminent. Glorification was on his mind. He asked the Father to glorify him, God's Son, that he might glorify God through giving eternal life to all whom God had given him. This was another claim to deity. He was thinking beyond the cross; it would be not the end of his life but the return to his Father to share again his glory accompanied by his redeemed people.

For His Glorification through his Life (17:4–5)

Jesus had glorified God on earth, doing his assigned work. He understood, from the beginning, his purpose to die as the atoning sacrifice for our sin. He came to save us from sin's penalty, power, and presence. Salvation from the penalty of sin means no more fear of death. Salvation from its power enables us to live a holy life. Salvation from its presence guarantees our glorified, sinless state in heaven. His purpose as a man was to offer himself in our place and on our behalf to make us fit to enter God's presence. He knew his God-given work and he knew he had done it perfectly.

Jesus asked God to give him the same glory in God's presence that he had before the world began. "Before His incarnation Jesus had possessed the fullness of God's attributes and character in the inward sense; He also possessed the fullness of God's outward, visible glory. In the Incarnation, Jesus laid the second of these aside; for, if He had not, we would not have been able to approach Him."[1] Jesus was filled with joy at the thought of returning to the Father and again sharing his glory.

As Jesus of Nazareth was crucified, he was also acquiring glory by perfectly fulfilling God's plan for him to be the sacrifice for sin. By completing his work, he would also glorify his Father in his perfect plan of redemption. Jesus anticipated heaven accompanied by

---

1. James Montgomery Boice, *The Gospel of John: Five Volumes in One* (Grand Rapids: Zondervan, 1985), 1105.

those the Father had given him. He returned exalted to the place of highest honor with a name that is above every name (Philippians 2:9). "Infinite glory cannot be increased, but this glory is greater in that there is now a greater understanding by both men and angels. Jesus' prayer for glory was answered, and someday every true believer will experience the dashing ecstasy of it."[2]

Jesus Prayed for His Disciples (John 17:6–19)

Jesus turned his attention to pray for his disciples, not the world. What joy filled his heart as he recounted that they received his words as God's words. They knew Jesus came from God and believed God sent him. However, it was one thing to follow him when he was visible; soon they would have to follow him when they could not see him. They would need right thinking, truth, protection, and growth in what it means to follow Jesus. Two relationships would define them.

Relationship with the World

How would they live in the world without withdrawing from it or conforming to it? Courage and steadfastness would be required to share in suffering to advance his kingdom. He asked God to keep them in his name, united to him and the Father. He wanted them to have the full measure of his joy. Until God was ready to take them out of the world, they would need his protection from the evil one.

Relationship with Each Other

How would these sometimes ambitious, impulsive, fearful, and confused men relate to one another? He asked God

2. R. Kent Hughes, *John: That You May Believe* (Wheaton, IL: Crossway Books, 1999), 394.

to sanctify them (set them apart and impart God's holiness to them) by the truth of God's Word. They had Jesus' example of being sent into the world; following him would be possible only through union with him. How would the world know that they came from the Father or that Jesus came and was in them? Jesus' consecration through his death would be passed on to them.

Jesus Prayed for All Believers (John 17:20–26)

Jesus then prayed for all those who would believe in him through the apostles' message. This included all believers for all subsequent ages.

Unity in Truth (17:20)

They must be united in their beliefs in the truth of his message. Jesus lived a perfect life, died for our sins on the cross, was raised by the Father for our justification, and ascended to the place of highest authority where he reigns and from where he will return. This gospel, and only this gospel, saves and unites us. It is accessible, written for us in the Bible.

How concerned are you for truth? Do you pray for people who have not yet been born—children, grandchildren, neighbors' children, and so on—to believe in Jesus through the gospel? What can you do to make this the central message from your church?

Unity with God and Christ (17:21–23)

The believers' union with God and Christ would demonstrate to the world that God sent Jesus. He prayed that believers might be perfectly one, giving testimony that God sent Jesus and loved them. This does not mean we all have to be alike. There is diversity in this unity. We are at different stages in life and different places in our walk with God.

Nigeria, Kenya, India, Australia, Brazil, Italy, France, England, Canada, Singapore . . . the experience was the same as I walked into a room of Bible Study Fellowship leaders. Immediately there was a sense of joy and unity between us, though we were different in age, nationality, spiritual maturity, educational level, and much more. We were God's answers to this prayer of Jesus for us. We were immediately one. Have you experienced such unity?

Eternal Destiny (17:24–26)

Finally, Jesus asked that believers would be with him where he is—with God in heaven. He wanted them to see his glory, which demonstrated God's eternal love for him. We will be able to see Jesus' glory because sin will no longer be present in us; we will also be glorified and will see Jesus as he is (1 John 3:2). Jesus promised to continue making the Father's name known to us and to all believers, that we might experience the Father's love as he had and live in union with him. Is this request in the Father's will? Absolutely! It describes the reason for which Jesus came. The joy of this hope has been and will be an anchor for his people amidst the trials of life.

Jesus prayed for all believers in every age. He was not praying for those who would refuse him as the only way to God. People cannot have unity with God unless they are in Christ. Was Jesus praying for you? How do you know? Can you know? Yes, this prayer teaches that those who believe in Jesus can have this assurance because Jesus has prayed for them. How does Jesus' prayer give you hope for the future and comfort for the present?

Agony in Gethsemane (Matthew 26:36–56; Mark 14:33–50; Luke 22:39–53)

From the elation of intimate prayer, Jesus moved to agonizing prayer. Leaving the upper room, Jesus and the disciples crossed the brook Kidron and went to a garden called Gethsemane on the Mount of Olives. He had gone there frequently. He told the disciples to sit down while he took Peter, James, and John to pray. He began to be greatly distressed and troubled, becoming very sorrowful, even to death. Before going a stone's throw away, he instructed them to watch and pray that they might not enter into temptation. His own comfort was not on his mind. He was not sitting in a comfortable chair or even kneeling with arms resting on a chair. He fell facedown before his Father.

His Prayer (Matthew 26:36–46; Mark 14:33–42; Luke 22:39–46)

Anticipating the Cup

We might think that Jesus, as true man, feared the emotional and physical pain of crucifixion. However, his first request of his Father showed that something far worse was on his mind. He faced "the cup" of God's holy wrath poured out against all sin. This cup was intended for all sinful humanity to drink (Psalm 75:8). Just a taste from this cup would make one stagger (Isaiah 51:17). Jesus would drink it to the dregs as he took our place as the object of God's full, furious, and righteous wrath. He faced the horror of being—not just feeling—forsaken by his Father (Mark 15:34) and of being utterly separated from intimacy with God and abandoned by him.

Pleading with His Father

He understood "the cup" from the Old Testament teaching (Psalm 22; Isaiah 53:4–10). He would experience the outpouring of God's wrath. He would not become a sinner; he would become sin and a curse! This overwhelmed him. His human agony was so intense that he fell on his face on the ground, and his sweat became like great drops of blood. An angel came from heaven to strengthen him. Nevertheless, acknowledging that all things were possible for his Father, he pled three times for an alternate way to satisfy God's wrath against sin. Was there another way for him to redeem those God had given him? Another way they could be with him in heaven? Each time, he concluded his request by submitting to his Father's will.

Three times he went away from the disciples to pray; each time he returned to find them asleep. Twice he admonished them to pray. The final time, he knew the time for prayer was over; the hour had come for the Son of Man to be betrayed. He said, "Rise, let us be going; see, my betrayer is at hand" (Matthew 26:46). He met the crowd with courage and steadfast faith in his Father.

Submitting to His Father's Plan

While Jesus was still speaking, Judas came leading a great, armed crowd from the chief priests, scribes, and elders. The hour of Jesus' betrayal, arrest, suffering, and crucifixion—the consummation of his work—was now. He was confident this was his Father's will. He would endure the agony of the next hours because of the anticipated joy beyond it.

Jesus demonstrated that prayer is more than a list of requests recited to God. Prayer can be agonizing as we seek to know and submit to God's will. God heard Jesus' requests because he was reverently submissive. God was pleased with his request (Psalm 22:24), but his answer was no. God strengthened his Son to face the horror of what was imminent. As a human, Jesus desired deliverance, but he was also given over completely to his Father's will. Also as a human, he learned obedience as he obeyed his Father through suffering (Hebrews 5:7–8).

God's will is that we embrace his purpose for us no matter the cost. We also learn obedience to God through agonizing in prayer and through joining our will to his.

His Arrest (Matthew 26:47–56; Mark 14:43–50; Luke 22:47–53; John 18:1–12)

His Dignity

Jesus stood in stark contrast to the approaching crowd. They were noisy, increasingly out of control. He was peaceful and calm. He faced his betrayer and the armed crowd with sovereign dignity. His actions showed that he was giving them permission to arrest him. He allowed Judas to kiss him, graciously calling him "friend." He approached them, asking whom they sought. When they answered, "Jesus of Nazareth," he responded, "I am he" (literally "I am"). His words were so powerful that they drew back and fell to the ground. They were unable to stand in the face of his power and majesty. A second time he asked whom they sought and identified himself as the one they had come to arrest.

His Compassion

Showing compassion toward his disciples, he offered himself but asked the crowd to let the disciples go. Without an argument, they obeyed him. When they laid hands on him to seize him, he stopped Peter from starting a riot by healing the ear of Malchus and telling Peter to put away his sword. How could the people miss this revelation of Jesus? Who but God could do this miracle of healing?

His Authority

Jesus could have appealed to his Father to send twelve legions (possibly twelve thousand legions) of angels to rescue them, but he did not. He would drink the cup that the Father had given him to fulfill the Scripture. He rebuked the crowd for coming under the cover of darkness and behind weapons when they could have approached him in the temple as he sat teaching. This, too, was the fulfillment of prophecy. He called it their "hour, and the power of darkness" (Luke 22:53). What a contrast to the hour of his glorification and the power of the cross that would bring life. With that, all the disciples left him and fled, leaving him to face the cross alone.

His Glory

Jesus resolved to bear all the imminent suffering. Nothing and no one would stop him—not Peter, Judas, the crowd, or anyone else. He faced the cross as his Father's will, not as the cruel whim of sinful humans. Against the backdrop of their evil intent and the power of darkness, Jesus radiated power, peaceful submission to his Father, grace to the wounded Malchus, protection of his own, and control of the crowd. He continued to demonstrate the message of the kingdom that he came to proclaim. He was more concerned for others than for himself. He brought glory to the Father even as he handed himself over. This was the predetermined will of God, the reason that he came. His glory in the face of such moral corruption, betrayal, denial, and cowardly cruelty is worthy of our love and worship.

What are your thoughts as you ponder that Jesus fully drank the cup that is your cup? I find it beneficial to think about deep truths each morning as I walk. No one is around me, the phone is out of hearing and reach, and my mind is occupied with eternal thoughts instead of "How much longer do I have to do this?" Where can you make time to ponder them? What can you learn from Jesus' prayers?

Jesus rejoiced in what he knew of God's plan of redemption. When he had finished his work, he knew he would be exalted. He would return in glory to be united with the Father, taking with him those he had redeemed. They would see him in his glory and be united with him and the Father. Do you rejoice in the anticipation of your glorification and this union? If so, thank God each day that your eternal destiny is secure.

You will never face a "Gethsemane"; Jesus has done it for you. He sweated great drops of blood, needing strength from an angel because of the enormity of God's wrath, which you deserve. You will never be an atoning sacrifice for sin. However, you may agonize in prayer, especially for loved ones to embrace the cross. Agonizing over a loved one, my friend prayed, "Lord, I would give my life if she would believe." The answer shocked her! "Your life is not good enough for that. The only one who could be the sacrifice for her sin already died in her place."

However, God may ask you to do something that will require "death to self" and to relinquish your comfort in order to submit your will to his. Following the Lord Jesus as you run God's race for you will mean that you pour out your heart to God for yourself and others—family members, church family, missionaries, political leaders, etc.

Kay's entire family had an unwelcome chapter added to their biography. "Life turned upside down and we were struck with excruciating pain when our daughter's husband announced he was leaving. As we were agonizing with her, we decided to look at the suffering Jesus went through at the cross and to view our suffering in light of his. We started looking to Jesus and away from our pain, keeping a daily list of the amazing things our God was doing for us as we cried out to him in prayer. She found an attorney late Friday afternoon and was in court Monday morning. She was back in her house with her children by Wednesday. Within two weeks, she sold her house along with everything she could not use, and found a job and a place to live. Our list is three pages long and growing. Keeping our eyes on God instead of our suffering, and looking to see what he would do each day, changed the weight of what we were bearing. God has revealed himself to us in amazing ways. Accepting what he has given us and keeping our eyes upon him truly gives us joy, which we offer to him and share with many unbelievers."

Prayer has different forms and purposes. It may be pure worship of God, recounting his attributes and his great work in our salvation (see Psalm 145). Prayer includes crying out in times of need. It is important to be real with God, honestly expressing agony to him (see Psalm 142), as Jesus did in Gethsemane. Prayer is a means of discerning God's will and submitting to it. Paul prayed three times for removal of a "thorn"; God said no but promised Paul sufficient grace to bear it (2 Corinthians 12:7–10).

Prayer anticipates God's faithfulness to his promises, presence, provision, grace, and power. How might your prayers change in light of Jesus' prayers before the cross?

Closing Prayer

O God, my Father, your plans and purposes for your children bring me to an entirely different perspective for my life. Life is about your glory and the eternal good of others. It is also about my union with you and my submission to you. Help me to learn from Jesus how to claim in prayer the truth that I am your gift to him. I know that my eternal destiny with you is secure, for you protect me from the evil one and Jesus continues to pray for me. I know I will be glorified—free from the presence of sin and like Jesus—in heaven. Help me learn to pour out my heart to you in prayer until I am able to rise from my knees and submit myself to you and your purposes for me. Let me remember my Savior and follow him. For his glory. Amen.

The Pain of the Cross

And he went out, bearing his own cross, to the place called The Place of a Skull, which in Aramaic is called Golgotha. There they crucified him. (John 19:17–18)

Texts

Psalm 22
Matthew 26–27
Mark 14:1–15:37
Luke 22–23
John 18–19

Truth

Because Jesus endured every kind of pain in our place, we are free to worship God and live for his glory without guilt and fear of his wrath.

Hymn: "Ah, Holy Jesus"

Ah, holy Jesus, how hast thou offended,
That man to judge thee hath in hate pretended?

By foes derided, by thine own rejected,
O most afflicted.

Who was the guilty? who brought this upon thee?
Alas, my treason, Jesus, hath undone thee.
'Twas I, Lord Jesus, I it was denied thee:
I crucified thee.

Lo, the Good Shepherd for the sheep is offered;
The slave hath sinned and the Son hath suffered:
For man's atonement, while he nothing heedeth,
God intercedeth.

For me, kind Jesus, was thine incarnation,
Thy mortal sorrow, and thy life's oblation:
Thy death of anguish and thy bitter passion,
For my salvation.

Therefore, kind Jesus, since I cannot pay thee,
I do adore thee, and will ever pray thee,
Think on thy pity and thy love unswerving,
Not my deserving.

—JOHANN HEERMANN, 1630

Opening Prayer

O God, our hearts are anguished as we consider what our sins cost our precious Savior. It is painful to think of his emotional and physical pain. Yet they were nothing compared to the agony of bearing our sins, becoming sin and a curse for us, and having your wrath poured out on him. We are grateful for your Holy Spirit, who helps us understand. Thank you for helping us to think deeply and for making us richer in our relationship with you. Teach us more about this important subject. Please give us grace to embrace the truth and embrace the cross, because it was for us that the Lord Jesus died. In his holy and mighty name. Amen.

Questions for Study and Discussion

► READ PSALM 22; MATTHEW 26–27; MARK 14:1–15:37; LUKE 22–23; JOHN 18–19

1. What accusations and actions were made against Jesus? Was Jesus treated justly? Why or why not?

2. How might Jesus have suffered because of the mocking?

3. How did Judas and Peter contribute to Jesus' pain? How can you avoid doing what they did?

4. Describe the physical pain to Jesus' human body as he approached the cross. See also Isaiah 50:6; 52:14.

5. Describe the physical details and pain of crucifixion.

6. What is the answer to Jesus' question, "My God, my God, why have you forsaken me?" See Psalm 22:1, 10–11, 19; Matthew 27:46; Isaiah 53:5, 6, 10; 2 Corinthians 5:21; Galatians 3:13; 1 Peter 2:24; 3:18.

7. Are you or someone you know experiencing the pain of abandonment or rejection? How does Jesus' being forsaken by his God and Father help you?

8. How has your understanding of the gravity of sin changed through pondering the necessity of Jesus' extreme suffering?

9. How would you describe yourself: "I am a sinner because I sin" or "I sin because I am a sinner"? How would your answer necessitate Jesus' being forsaken by his God and becoming sin and a curse?

10. What would your life be like if Jesus had not endured the pain of the cross for you?

11. In what specific ways might Jesus' pain help you when you are falsely accused, unjustly treated, denied, or betrayed?

12. Meditate on your answers, the Scripture references, and the words of "Ah, Holy Jesus." Use them to write a prayer of worship and commitment to God the Father and the Lord Jesus Christ.

Commentary

What sort of pain have you suffered, or observed in the life of another? My mother died unexpectedly the day after Christmas, two weeks after I became engaged, eight months before I married. Her absence at my wedding was deeply felt by all.

I have watched healthy loved ones die unexpectedly. The process of dying was agonizingly slow and painful for others. Some suffer through rejection by a loved one. A child's foolish choices cause deep heartache for an entire family. The death of a spouse leaves someone alone. Abandonment by a spouse or child creates deep scars. Deep agony results from false accusations with no opportunity for self-defense. Termination by an employer with no advance warning can be devastating.

The guilt of the past can hang over your head and make you wonder why God does not seem to answer. The consequences of sinful choices remain. You cry out to God and things seem to get worse instead of better. These true examples of life can cause deep emotional and sometimes physical pain and spiritual agony.

There is agony that surpasses these examples. It was the agony of Jesus Christ as he atoned for all the sins of his people. The reason he came to earth was to die. The emotional and physical shame and suffering were intense for this true man with a real human body; yet the spiritual agony he endured was far worse, more than our finite minds can comprehend.

It is painful to look closely at his suffering. Yet it benefits us to ponder it so we can understand something of its intensity and intent. It reveals God's justice, holiness, and view of sin. It also shows us God's love demonstrated to us while we were still sinners (Romans 5:8). Only when we have right facts and study them diligently will we have right thinking that leads to mature faith. Jesus endured every kind of pain in our place, so we are free to worship God without guilt and fear of his wrath.

Many in our culture are desensitized to pain and suffering. We watch the evening news and are unaffected by reports of murder or other local and global violence. We watch live action in war zones without being startled by the sight of brutal death.

Have you been to a movie and wept as others laughed and were entertained by it? Or did you laugh along with the crowd? How are you becoming desensitized to pain and suffering?

You may have shed tears as you studied this lesson; that is good because it shows that you are not desensitized. The narrative has not become so familiar that you can quickly skim over the details and resume your normal activities without a second thought. Let us not run from Jesus' suffering because it is hard. Let us not shut down emotionally as we look at our Savior and the agony he endured on his way to the cross. But let us also remember his euphoria in completing his Father's will through what he suffered. His triumph through suffering belongs to his redeemed people.

Emotional Pain

Prior to His Crucifixion

Jesus wrestled in prayer in Gethsemane before facing those who came to arrest him. After a sleepless night, Jesus was dragged before religious and political authorities and falsely accused. He, the Lawgiver, faced six trials that were unjust on every account. He faced them with courage and silence. He was perfectly innocent, without guilt or sin, and yet was associated with everything vile and wicked. He, the Prince of Peace, was accused of circumventing Roman authority. He, the Son of God, was accused of blasphemy.

Jesus responded with silence to vicious mockery concerning the very roles that were rightfully his—prophet, priest, and king. The temptation to skip the cross increased through this mocking. The self-righteous religious leaders tore their clothes in protest, yet spat in his face when he answered truthfully that he was the

Messiah, the Son of God. They blindfolded him and told him to say who struck him, mocking him as prophet. The soldiers railed at him, placing a scepter in his hand and hailing him as King, which he was and is. He, the High Priest who would sacrifice his own body for his people, could not avoid this suffering of being stripped, spat upon, and mocked with sarcasm and vicious words. His own people asked to have Barabbas, a convicted insurrection-ist and murderer, released instead of Jesus. Jesus, the sinless one, died in place of Barabbas, who was set free. What a picture of atonement! Do you see yourself in this picture?

His only answer during the interrogation was to affirm him-self as the promised Messiah, the Son of God. Failure to do so would have denied his person. Could he have insisted on his innocence? No! The agony of suffering in silence when falsely accused of blasphemy, lying, and sedition could not be avoided. He had to fulfill the Scripture (Isaiah 53:7). He had determined in Gethsemane to drink the cup of God's wrath that we deserve. If he had defended himself, he would not have experienced our shame, leaving us guilty. If he had not fulfilled God's purpose for him, he would have none to follow him to heaven, and we would have no hope of eternal life.

What guilt and shame are you experiencing today? If you are God's child through faith in Christ, he bore them in your place. For you to continue to live under their tyranny is to deny that Christ's suffering was enough. What can you possibly add to it?

On the Cross

Crucifixion was a slow and painful execution in which the condemned person was nailed or tied to a cross and left to die. Crucifixion was normally reserved for the basest criminals, so Jesus was put down to the lowest level. He was forced to carry his cross along the road to the death site outside the city. Everyone along the way would think he was a criminal being put to death for his own sins. The death would be in view of both passersby along the road and curious onlookers from the city. His name would forever be associated with the infamy of crucifixion. To hang naked on the cross would have been extremely humiliating in the Jewish culture.

Where were his closest friends? They were absent or afar except for his mother, Mary, and his beloved disciple, John. He was alone and abandoned—the thing most of us fear more than anything.

Psalm 22:6–18 prophesied that Jesus would be a worm, scorned, despised, mocked, and derided for his faith in God, with trouble near and none to help. Those intent on evil were described as bulls, a ravenous and roaring lion, and ferocious dogs. Can you picture these people snarling, like a pit bull dog baring its teeth at you? Jesus may have been praying, "Do not be far off . . . come quickly to my aid! Deliver my soul from the sword, my precious life from the power of the dog! Save me" (Psalm 22:19–21). His suffering was real and exactly as prophesied.

What kind of emotion would the treatment that Jesus endured arouse in you? How do you react when you experience embarrassment or abandonment or when you doubt that God cares for you and will do for you as he promised? How quick are you to defend yourself in the face of angry, false accusations or to run from difficulties related to being a Christian? Do you want to deny Christ, like Peter, or betray him, like Judas? What joy might await you as you silently endure the agony of the moment, trusting God to take care of you and to use it for his glory and your eternal good? Sometimes it is best not to have the last word in a conversation.

Physical Pain

Prior to the Cross

When Jesus was interrogated by Pontius Pilate, the people demanded that Barabbas be released instead of Jesus. Although Pilate found Jesus guilty of none of the charges against him, he said, "I will therefore punish and release him" (Luke 23:16). Why beat someone who was not guilty?

Jesus was beaten twice—before being sentenced to death (Luke 23:16; John 19:1) and after (Matthew 27:26; Mark 15:15).[1] The initial flogging was probably the type administered for minor crimes.[2] After the flogging, Jesus was beaten and slapped by Roman soldiers saying, "Hail, King of the Jews!" They spat on him, pulled out his beard, repeatedly struck him on his head with a staff, shoved him around, put a purple robe on him, and pushed a crown of thorns onto his head (Matthew 27:27–31).

After the sentencing, the scourging that took place was reserved for capital punishments, including crucifixion. The condemned was "tied to a post and beaten with a leather whip that was interwoven with pieces of bone and metal, which tore through skin and tissue, often exposing bones and intestines."[3] This also caused deep bruising or contusions. His back became a bloody mass of ground-up flesh. They mocked him, struck his head again, and put the robe back on him. How that rough robe must have inflamed his wounded back. Then they tied the cross bar to his arms to carry to the place of crucifixion, Golgotha.

1. Taken from study note on John 19:1 in the *ESV® Study Bible* (The Holy Bible, *English Standard Version®*), copyright 2008 by Crossway, a publishing ministry of Good News Publishers.

2. Ibid.

3. Taken from study note on Matthew 27:26 in ibid.

Imagine the pain as the bar rubbed across his severely beaten back. By this time, Jesus was so weakened that they called a passerby, Simon of Cyrene, to carry the cross bar for him.

Do you say, "Those horrible Jewish leaders, those brutal Roman soldiers—how could they do that to Jesus?" It was not just they; it was all of us, too. God planned for Jesus to die in this way for our sin (Acts 2:23). What does that tell you about the heinousness of your sin and the enormousness of God's love for you? Make a list of the sins that you contributed to Jesus' suffering. Will you take time to thank God for his forgiveness of each one?

On the Cross

Jesus refused a narcotic drink to dull his pain. He must experience the full agony involved in carrying the punishment for our sins. He lay on the cross bar to be nailed to the cross. These were not small nails but probably heavy wrought iron spikes, possibly 5–10 inches (12.7–25.4 cm) long. They were driven between the wrist bones to avoid fracture but would crush longer bones in the arms, causing intense pain.

Psalm 22:14–17 describes some of the physical effects of crucifixion: a feeling of emptiness like poured-out water, bones out of joint, heart like melted wax, strength dried up, tongue sticking to the jaw, pierced hands and feet, bones countable as people seemed to stare at him and gloat over him. His bones poked through his skin as they went out of joint. He had no strength or energy. He could not breathe easily due to his position on the cross.

There was a footrest to keep his body from tearing loose from the cross. As he tried to push up on his feet to alleviate the stress to his torso, the pain to his entire body would be excruciating.

To hasten death, the soldiers would break the legs, making it impossible to push up to breathe. The arm strength would fail and asphyxiation would follow. However, Jesus' legs were not broken. He did not die from asphyxiation but by giving up his spirit to God. His pierced side showed that he was dead.

As a true man, Christ suffered emotional and physical pain on the way to, and on, the cross. However, all who were crucified experienced pain. Martyrs also suffered other grotesque methods of execution.[4] We look at Jesus' emotional and physical sufferings because they help us to understand the greatness of his spiritual suffering. His death on the cross was like no other death—it was an atoning sacrifice for sin.

Spiritual Pain

We cannot completely grasp Jesus' spiritual pain. However, Scripture puts words to his agony. Remember Jesus' prayer in John 17, where he joyfully anticipated his eternal glory in heaven with his Father and those redeemed by his death. Their union was the assurance of his victory. He had trusted God as his God even as a nursing infant (Psalm 22:9–10). As a man, he drew hope from that union and from the joy of praising God in the great congregation of the redeemed from all the nations, even to the ends of the earth (Psalm 22:22–31). Yet, Jesus said to his disciples in Gethsemane, "My soul is very sorrowful, even to death" (Matthew 26:38), expressing the horror of separation from his Father.

After Jesus fasted forty days following his baptism, Satan tempted Jesus, the Man, to claim his kingdom without endur-

4. John Foxe, *Foxe's Book of Martyrs* (John Day, 1563; repr. Peabody, MA: Hendrickson Publishers, 2004).

ing the cross (Matthew 4:1–11). At other "opportune times," he tried to lure Jesus into choosing a path that would avoid the cross (Luke 4:13). At the cross, he used the taunts of the crowd to tempt Jesus into coming down to prove he was the promised Messiah and Son of God. The spiritual forces of evil surrounded Jesus in this final attempt to stop God's purpose for his life. Yet no spiritual assault could thwart God's purpose for the cross.

Jesus faced the cup of God's just and righteous wrath against sin. He was willingly forsaken by God and unable to communicate with him. He was separated from his Father, abandoned by his God. His suffering was unmerited; he did nothing to warrant this outpouring of God's wrath. He was righteous, had no sin, and was always perfectly obedient to his Father.

As prophesied, Jesus cried out, "My God, my God, why have you forsaken me?" (Psalm 22:1; Matthew 27:46). Wherever we put the emphasis (my, God, why, you, me), the intensity of the pain remains the same. The only perfect one who always obeyed and submitted to God the Father suffered the agony of hell. He did not just feel forsaken; he was forsaken. This pain eclipsed his physical and emotional pain. Who can understand this spiritual agony?

Why did he have to suffer? What was the reason for this agony? God planned our redemption this way, knowing what it would take to turn his wrath away from us. It was God's will for him to suffer in our place (Isaiah 53:5–10). We deserved to be cursed for breaking God's law, but he became a curse for us to redeem us from the curse of the law (Galatians 3:13). He suffered on our behalf. "He himself bore our sins in his body on the tree, that we might die to sin and live to righteousness" (1 Peter 2:24). He did not become a sinner. He, the only sinless human, became sin for us that we might become the righteousness of God (2 Corinthians 5:21).

What does the pain on the cross tell you about God the Father? First, your sin is no small matter to God. He hates sin and cannot ignore it. As the righteous Judge and holy God, he must deal rightly with sin or deny himself. "The wages of sin is death" (Romans 6:23), so someone must die for your sin and mine. Do you hate sin like God does? It is easy to hate the sin of another, but what about your sin? Second, God's love is no small thing either. He loved you enough to save you at great cost from the eternal destruction that you deserve (Romans 5:8). Jesus was willing to suffer so you and I could escape God's wrath. He was willing to suffer because he came to do his Father's will.

> What difference does Jesus' suffering make in your life? Daphne's husband of many years announced that he was moving out. Sadly, she is not unique among Christians. What has enabled her to go through the pain of abandonment and rejection?
>
> "It hurts in a profound way to be abandoned and forsaken by someone I trusted and truly love. Yet my pain is nothing compared to what Jesus experienced in my place. I did not choose to be abandoned, but Jesus chose to be left by God and God chose to forsake his only Son for me, a wretched sinner. Jesus was silent for all the tortures, but not this one. Jesus cried out to God in response to the greatest pain he had ever felt, 'My God, my God, why have you forsaken me?' (Mark 15:34). But there was no answer. God abandoned him on purpose in his time of greatest human need. Their perfect communion and love, uninterrupted for all eternity past, was broken. Jesus was forsaken of everything loving and holy as God turned his face away from him. His death included everything evil that Satan could throw at him, and God the Father poured out his wrath, which I deserve, on

his only Son to save me. Why did God forsake Jesus? I am the answer to that question. God was forsaking Jesus for me. What a Savior!"

Seeing the cross from God's perspective provides her with comfort, strength, and joy even in the midst of the agony of rejection. When faced with this agony, she could have shaken her fist in anger at God. Understanding Jesus' pain for her, she ran instead into his loving embrace.

What Does the Cross Tell Us about Ourselves?

Observing the agony and horror of the cross that Jesus endured for us, we begin to glimpse the gravity of our sin. Your sins and mine put Jesus on the cross. He became sin, became a curse, and bore our sins in his body because we are helpless to save ourselves. He was stripped naked that you and I might be clothed with his perfect, sinless life. This means we have power to live as he did. In place of fear and doubt, we can trust God's promises and purposes for us.

It is hard to admit our true state: we are not sinners because we sin; we sin because we are sinners. We are not basically good and occasionally do bad things; we are basically bad. In fact, we are dead in sin (Ephesians 2:1). Dead people do not crawl out of the grave to help themselves. Yet God loved us in that helpless condition and demonstrated his love by sending Christ to die for us (1 John 4:10). While we have not committed every possible sin, we all have within us the potential to do so. Theologians call this "total depravity."

It is humbling to admit that you can do nothing to remove the guilt of your sin; you need someone else to do it on your behalf. The more you understand your depravity, the more you see how much God loves you. Your sin is like a black velvet backdrop to display the brilliance of the diamond of Christ's love demonstrated by his death in your place and on your behalf. As you ponder your sin and Christ's love, do not be dragged down with self-absorption in guilt and self-deprecation. Take the free gift of his righteousness and eternal life. Move on to love and worship Jesus for what he did on the cross.

Because Jesus endured every kind of pain in your place, you are free to worship God and live for his glory without guilt and fear of his wrath. Think about and write down how gloriously different your life is because Jesus Christ died for you. Turn your thoughts into prayers of adoration and thanksgiving to God. Also, use the Scriptures, truths, and hymns we have learned.

Closing Prayer

Holy Jesus, hateful men thought they could judge you although you had committed no offense. I grieve that you were ridiculed by your foes, rejected by your own people, and most afflicted. Yet I crucified you by my betrayal and denial. You, the Good Shepherd, offered yourself as my sacrificial lamb. You, the Son, suffered for me, the slave. O Jesus, you intervened as mediator reconciling me to God while I ignored my need for reconciliation. Kind Jesus, for me you became a man, lived a sorrowful life, and offered your holy sacrifice; you endured bitter passion and an anguishing death for my salvation. I cannot repay you, but I adore you for dying in my place and on my behalf. Help me never to think that I deserved this enormous expression of love. Yet help me to accept it and worship you because of your pity and love. May I not become self-absorbed or carry around my guilt; may I see my sins and guilt on you and walk in the newness of life that you bought for me. For your glory. Amen. (Based on "Ah, Holy Jesus")

The Perfection of the Cross

But when Christ appeared as a high priest of the good things that have come, then through the greater and more perfect tent (not made with hands, that is, not of this creation) he entered once for all into the holy places, not by means of the blood of goats and calves but by means of his own blood, thus securing an eternal redemption. (Hebrews 9:11–12)

Texts

Leviticus 16
Hebrews 7–10

Truth

Jesus, the perfect High Priest, forgave our sin and removed our guilt by offering himself, the only perfect sacrifice for sin.

Hymn: "Nothing But the Blood of Jesus"

What can wash away my sin?
Nothing but the blood of Jesus;
What can make me whole again?
Nothing but the blood of Jesus.

Refrain:
O precious is the flow
That makes me white as snow;
No other fount I know,
Nothing but the blood of Jesus.

For my cleansing this I see—
Nothing but the blood of Jesus;
For my pardon this my plea—
Nothing but the blood of Jesus. *Refrain*

Nothing can for sin atone—
Nothing but the blood of Jesus;
Naught of good that I have done—
Nothing but the blood of Jesus. *Refrain*

This is all my hope and peace—
Nothing but the blood of Jesus;
This is all my righteousness—
Nothing but the blood of Jesus. *Refrain*

Now by this I'll overcome—
Nothing but the blood of Jesus;
Now by this I'll reach my home—
Nothing but the blood of Jesus. *Refrain*

—ROBERT LOWRY, 1876

Opening Prayer

O Lord, our God, nothing but the blood of Jesus can atone for our sin, forgive us of our sins, wash away the guilt of our sins, and enable us to live a new life. Help us by the power of your Word and Holy Spirit to understand that only Jesus could offer the perfect sacrifice of atonement. He not only paid for our sins that we might be forgiven, but he also removed the guilt of them so that we might live in an entirely new way for your glory and honor and for the furtherance of your kingdom. In Jesus' name, Amen.

Questions for Study and Discussion

▶ READ LEVITICUS 16:1–20

1. List what the high priest was required to do on the Day of Atonement.

2. What did you find interesting about these required offerings?

▶ READ LEVITICUS 16:5, 15–22

3. Describe the two offerings that the high priest made for the people.

a. The first goat (Leviticus 16:15–19; see also 4:27–31)

b. The second goat (Leviticus 16:20–22)

4. Why would God prescribe this type of sacrifice for sin?
    See Hebrews 9:22.

▶ **READ HEBREWS 7**

5. How is Jesus different from Aaron and other high priests? See also Hebrews 2:17; 4:15–16.

6. Why is this difference important for Jesus' followers?

▶ READ HEBREWS 8:2; 9:11–14, 24

7. How is the place of Jesus' sacrifice different from the tabernacle?

8. How do the two goats on the Day of Atonement point to what Jesus accomplished for you when he died on the cross? Use any passage of Scripture for your answer.

9. Why is it important to understand the Day of Atonement and its relationship to the cross of Christ?

10. How would your life be different if you had to sacrifice animals for your sin?

11. How does Jesus' perfect sacrifice assure you that God forgives your sins and removes your guilt? What difference does that make in your daily life?

12. Describe living without guilt. Give specific examples. Does this describe you?

13. Study the words of the hymn "Nothing but the Blood of Jesus." How do they help you to understand the perfection of Jesus' sacrificial death?

Commentary

Perhaps you have tried to read through the entire Bible. The exciting stories in Genesis and Exodus held your attention. Then you got to Leviticus. You waded through the first two chapters, but by the third you gave up. Your reading plan was aborted. You are not alone! However, studying Leviticus is worth the effort it takes. Leviticus will help you to understand more deeply what Jesus did for you and to realize that every word of Scripture is "profitable for teaching, for reproof, for correction, and for training in righteousness, that the man of God may be competent, equipped for every good work" (2 Timothy 3:16–17).

God explained his plan for redeeming his people. Many of our plans go awry because imperfect people make them. God's plans are always perfect because he is perfect. He planned the perfect way for our sins to be forgiven and the perfect way for us to be free from bearing our load of guilt. This lesson focuses on the Day of Atonement (Leviticus 16), which points to Jesus' perfect sacrifice.

Atonement is the act whereby sinful man can be reconciled to a holy God. This plan for atonement was God's idea. He determined the details of it. Then he carried them out. Our ideas will never be better. Do you think you can be acceptable to God by working hard, by being sincere, by faithful church attendance, by giving a tithe and more? Your efforts may be commendable, but they will not earn God's love and favor. They are not enough to forgive your sins or massage your guilt so it will go away even for a while. That is not the way God planned for forgiveness and removal of guilt. Your efforts will not bridge the gap that your sin caused between you and God, nor will they remove the guilt you carry.

Why waste time on what will never work? It behooves us to understand God's plan in the big picture of both the Old and New Testaments. Atonement was anticipated by the Old Testament and was fulfilled in Christ's perfect sacrifice. Leviticus 16 and Hebrews 7–10 help us understand the defining moment in all of history when Jesus, the perfect High Priest, offered himself, the only perfect atonement for sin.

Anticipated by the Old Testament Day of Atonement (Leviticus 16)

Purpose of the Day of Atonement

God's way of atonement for the nation of Israel anticipated how we receive atonement in Christ. Once a year, the high priest offered specified sacrifices to God on the Day of Atonement (Leviticus 16:2–22, 34). God established the Day of Atonement so that the people of Israel would understand their sin and need of a Savior. The day also provided them a temporary way to return to God until Christ the Savior came. Blood had to be sprinkled on everything and everyone needing atonement—the high priest, the priests and people, the tent of meeting, the Holy Place, and the altar. All were unclean because of their contact with the sins of the people. Each must be cleansed in the proper order.

Imperfection of the Day of Atonement Sacrifice

The priest offering the sacrifice was imperfect. The priest had to offer a sacrifice for his own sin before offering the sacrifice for the people. He also had limited access to God (Leviticus 16:2). Before he could even enter the Most Holy Place, he had to put incense on the fire to create a "cloud" or fog above the mercy seat to prevent and protect him from seeing the presence of God clearly (16:12–14).[1] He had to wash to be clean and put on special garments before he could present the offering to God. He was not a lasting priest; he would die and others would follow him.

The place of the offering was imperfect. The place of the offering was defiled by the sins of the people. Before the priest could offer sacrifices, he had to offer cleansing for the Holy Place, tent of meeting, and altar (16:16–19). After the cleansing, no one was allowed in the tent until the sacrifice had been completed.

1. Taken from study note on Leviticus 16:11–17 in the *ESV® Study Bible* (The Holy Bible, *English Standard Version®*), copyright 2008 by Crossway, a publishing ministry of Good News Publishers.

Only after making atonement for the place of offering would he present the sacrificial animal (16:20).

The sacrifices were imperfect. Two goats were offered. One was the sin offering for the forgiveness of sin (16:15). It was a substitute for the people, dying in their place so God could forgive them. It would represent *propitiation*—God's turning aside his wrath by turning it onto the goat. The priest would slit its throat, proving that it was dead. It had to be killed so that its blood could be poured on the altar (16:18). Imagine the noise and smell! Why would God demand such a gross offering? He was teaching the nation the ugliness of sin and what would be required to forgive them—the shedding of blood. The physical act of killing the goat and shedding its blood was to teach people what Christ would experience on the cross. His blood would be shed in a brutal way—crucifixion. An animal cannot bear your guilt and mine because it is not human and hence has no potential for guilt; only a man who faced temptation without sinning could be a sufficient sacrifice. Jesus Christ, a man, could! Jesus was the only man who could, because he was the only sinless man.

The second goat represented *expiation*, the removal of the guilt of sin. It was called the "scapegoat" (16:8, 10, 20–22, 26, KJV and other versions). When Aaron, the high priest, finished atonement for himself, the holy place, the altar, and the tent of meeting, he brought forward the guilt offering. As he put his hand on the head of the goat, he confessed his sins and the sins of the nation. By his confession, the sins passed from him to the head of the goat. It was taken outside the camp by a designated person and turned loose to wander in the wilderness to die, taking their guilt far away from them.

What a beautiful picture of how God removed our guilt through Christ, our scapegoat.

Perfection of Christ's Sacrifice—Hebrews 7–10

God prescribed the exact manner in which the sacrifices were to be offered on the Day of Atonement. He also prescribed the hour, way, person (the high priest), place, and perfect sacrifice for complete removal of our sin and guilt. Jesus of Nazareth, the Son of God, died on a cross outside Jerusalem. Peter declared, "This Jesus, delivered up according to the definite plan and foreknowledge of God, you crucified and killed by the hands of lawless men" (Acts 2:23). God's way of atonement is not open for discussion, debate, or opinion. What makes it a perfect sacrifice?

The High Priest Is Perfect

Jesus, the High Priest, was a true man so he could represent us (Hebrews 2:17). He was "holy, innocent, unstained, separated from sinners" and "made perfect forever" (7:26, 28). He was humanly tempted, as we are, yet without sin (4:15); therefore, he needed no sacrifices for himself. He is able to sympathize with us in our weakness and to offer us mercy and grace in our need.

His priesthood is permanent since he continues forever (7:17, 23–24). The sacrifices of animals were never enough. His once-for-all sacrifice was enough "to save to the uttermost those who draw near to God through him"; we will not fall because our High Priest constantly intercedes on our behalf (7:25). His blood pleads for us. Exalted above the heavens, he has unlimited access to God the Father (7:26). He offered himself once for all; his sacrifice was eternal (7:27; 9:12).

The Place of Sacrifice Is Perfect

The place of Jesus' sacrifice was set up by the Lord, not man (Hebrews 8:2; 9:11). It is heaven itself, not a copy of it (9:24). It is the place where God dwells. It needed no cleansing since sinful people cannot go in and out of it.

The Sacrifice Is Perfect

Jesus perfectly fulfilled God's requirement for a substitutionary blood sacrifice by a blameless human. He was both the perfect sin offering and the perfect scapegoat.

First, he is the perfect sin offering. He was unblemished because he remained sinless though he was tempted in every way (Hebrews 4:15). The sin of his people was transferred onto him, the sin offering (Isaiah 53:6; 1 Peter 2:24). His human blood, not an animal's blood, was shed as he died on the cross. Jesus had to become a man so that he could be a blood sacrifice for our sins. He entered into the Holy Place, the very presence of God, with his blood, opening the way for us to enter God's presence (Hebrews 9:11–12; 10:19–20).

The Old Testament sacrifice was a reminder of sin, but immediately the priest had to prepare for the next one. Jesus' perfect sacrifice was offered one time only; it does not need to be repeated (Hebrews 9:23–28; 10:1–4, 11–14). Jesus' sacrifice had perfect results, accomplishing God's intended purpose. His blood was the payment (ransom) that God required for our eternal redemption from bondage to sin (Mark 10:45). Jesus' blood cleansed our hearts, not just our behavior (Hebrews 9:13–14; 10:14–18). God laid on Jesus all our sins of the past, the present, and the future in that defining moment in history when he died.

Second, he is the perfect scapegoat. If our sins are on us, we are guilty and have to die. If, by faith, our sins are on Jesus, he died in our place. He chose to take our sins on him so that we would no longer carry the guilt for them. Furthermore, God remembers our sins no more (Hebrews 10:17). Our omniscient God always knows all things, including our sins. However, he chooses not to bring them up against us; he has already laid them on Christ. Jesus paid the full price to satisfy God's righteous judgment against them.

God requires no more offering for sin or guilt. Christ's death provides full assurance of faith and confidence to hold onto God's promises in him (Hebrews 10:22–23).

The Transfer of Sin and Guilt

Where are your sins? On you or on Jesus? Someone must die to receive the wages that your sin deserves (Romans 6:23). Jesus' sacrificial death turned God's wrath away from you by placing it on Jesus. Have you by faith seen your sin (past, present, future) on Jesus?

Who is carrying your guilt? You or Jesus? Will you trust God that Jesus carried your guilt away from you forever? Perhaps you think, "There is no way that could work for me. The things I have done or failed to do are too bad. No one could ever erase them from my memory." To continue carrying your own guilt is to declare that Jesus' sacrifice was not enough. Who are you to declare that what God considers sufficient is insufficient for you?

It is not God who continually brings up our sins against us. Our enemy, the Devil, accuses us and bombards us with guilt so that we are not free to love God, worship God, serve God, or tell others about him. Satan's list of our sins is accurate, but he carefully omits God's grace in Christ. Martin Luther is said to have listed his sins on a piece of paper. Then he wrote across the top, "Covered by the blood of Jesus." After agonizing for years, he was freed from the heavy load of guilt. Will you make a list of sins you have committed or good things you have omitted, and then write over it, "covered by the blood of Jesus"? See them on Christ when he died in your place and on your behalf. His sacrificial offering was enough to forgive you and to carry away your guilt. Will you believe this and live in the light of it?

What does it look like to live without guilt? Jesus' perfect sacrifice was sufficient to atone for your sin and guilt. However, there is more good news. God credited Christ's righteousness to those who trust him as Savior (Romans 3:22). If you have believed what the Bible says about Christ's atoning sacrifice, you have his perfect life to empower you to live in a new way that glorifies God. You are free to live without regret or shame. If you have confessed your sins to God, he has both forgiven you for them and removed them from you. In their place, you can be filled with his joy and peace instead of wrestling with the agony of guilt. You can experience the assurance of God's love instead of doubting how he could possibly love you. You can also enjoy the freedom to love him wholeheartedly in response to what he has done to show you his love.

In Christ, you are irrevocably adopted into God's family; you are given the Holy Spirit to live in you to guide, strengthen, comfort, and empower you (Galatians 4:6–7). Nothing you can do will make God love you more; he has already demonstrated his incomparable love for you in Christ. Nothing you can do will ever make God love you less; nothing and no one, even you, will be able to separate you from God's love in Christ Jesus (Romans 8:31–39). In our world of fear, loneliness, and insecurity, you can shine like a light. God's love is perfect, like every part of him.

When I started to study the Bible, I felt I had failed miserably as a Christian, a professional, and a mother. I was weary of missing the mark. I felt the heavy burden of my sins. I wanted to please God but increasingly became aware I could not.

I read the entire gospel of Matthew one afternoon. The first time God ever spoke to me through his Word was in Matthew 11:28–30: "Come to me, all who labor and are heavy laden, and I will give you rest. Take my yoke upon you, and learn from me, for I am gentle and lowly in heart, and you will find rest for your souls. For my yoke is easy, and my burden is light." This was good news! I continued reading and was horrified by the seven woes addressed to the Pharisees in Matthew 23. They described me! As I confessed my sin, Jesus' gracious call stirred me to be yoked to him. He has confirmed the truth of this promise for more than forty years, guiding me through circumstances I would not have chosen. He is perfect, and I am not. His perfect sacrifice will always meet my need.

What is a reasonable response to the perfection of Christ and his sacrifice? Close your eyes and think about Jesus, nailed to the cross on Golgotha. Your perfect High Priest is carrying his own perfect blood into the presence of his Father in the perfect tabernacle in heaven. This could be your story: "Jesus died for my sins. He took away my guilt. God gave me Christ's perfect life to empower me. I will not carry the guilt of my sins, because Jesus already did. I trust that his sacrifice was perfect and sufficient to remove my guilt. I will not dishonor him by continuing to live under guilt."

But what can you do when thoughts of guilt recur? Run to the cross! Stop and picture the scene at Golgotha again. Repeat your reasonable response to Christ's sacrifice for you. Replace the Devil's lies by filling your mind with the truth of Christ's perfect sacrifice. Remember through the Lord's Supper what Christ did for you by his broken body and shed blood. Walk away in newness of life in Christ.

You may be thinking that your sin was beyond forgiveness. It was a "big one." Jesus' blood covered all your sins: fear, doubt, adultery, murder, slander, rage, and all the others. Run to the cross each time you find yourself feeling guilty and too bad to be forgiven, as well as each time you feel that you are too "good" to need God's forgiveness.

What can wash away your sins? Nothing but the blood of Jesus!

Closing Prayer

Lord God, you are perfect in every way. Your plan for atonement is perfect. Nothing can be added to it; nothing can be taken from it. Every part of it is necessary, and every part of it is sufficient. Help me not to grieve unnecessarily with false guilt; but when I am truly guilty, help me not to let it become a burden. Help me remember that Jesus took my guilt from me when he died in my place and on my behalf. May I truly walk in the freedom that is mine in him. May I help others do the same. Amen.

The People at the Cross

Standing by the cross of Jesus were his mother and his mother's sister, Mary the wife of Clopas, and Mary Magdalene. When Jesus saw his mother and the disciple whom he loved standing nearby, he said to his mother, "Woman, behold, your son!" Then he said to the disciple, "Behold, your mother!" And from that hour the disciple took her to his own home. (John 19:25–27)

Texts

Matthew 27:36–56
Mark 15:21–41
Luke 23:26–49
John 19:18–27

Truth

Near the cross is a place of intimacy and great blessing.

Hymn: "Beneath the Cross of Jesus"

Beneath the cross of Jesus I fain would take my stand,
The shadow of a mighty Rock within a weary land;
A home within the wilderness, a rest upon the way,
From the burning of the noontide heat and the burden
    of the day.

Upon the cross of Jesus mine eye at times can see
The very dying form of One who suffered there for me:
And from my stricken heart with tears two wonders I
    confess,
The wonders of redeeming love and my unworthiness.

I take, O cross, thy shadow for my abiding place:
I ask no other sunshine than the sunshine of his face;
Content to let the world go by, to know no gain nor loss;
My sinful self my only shame, my glory all the cross.

—Elizabeth C. Clephane (1830–1869), 1872

Opening Prayer

Lord God, thank you for the gift of hymn writers who have taken their place beneath the cross of Jesus. Would you teach us by your Word and Spirit what it means to take our place beneath the cross? May we find that the cross provides rest, assurance of your love, and intimacy with you. In Jesus' name. Amen.

Questions for Study and Discussion

▶ READ MATTHEW 27:39–40 AND MARK 15:29–30

1. How did the people who passed by respond to Jesus on the cross?

2. Give examples of how people today respond to Jesus and his death in similar ways.

3. Describe your responses to Jesus and his death.

▶ READ MATTHEW 27:41–43; MARK 15:31–32; LUKE 23:35; AND JOHN 19:20–22

4. Explain the response of the Jewish religious leaders to Jesus on the cross.

5. How are people today like them?

6. How are you like them?

▶ READ MATTHEW 27:38, 44; MARK 15:32;
AND LUKE 23:39–43

7. What were the responses of the two men crucified next to Jesus?

8. What personal warning or encouragement do you receive from their responses?

▶ READ MATTHEW 27:32–37, 54; MARK 15:21–27, 39;
LUKE 23:33–38; AND JOHN 19:17–24

9. Describe the attitude and response of the Roman soldiers
to Jesus as they crucified him.

10. How did they change when Jesus died?

11. What do you learn from the Roman soldiers about evaluating the historical evidence of Christ's death? How careful are you to examine it?

▶ READ MATTHEW 27:55–56; MARK 15:40–41; LUKE 23:49; AND JOHN 19:25–27

12. Who were the different groups of Jesus' followers at the cross?

13. What do you learn about Jesus from his interaction with Mary and John that is applicable to you?

14. Explain what it means to be "near the cross." Use the words of the hymn "Beneath the Cross of Jesus" to help you.

15. How would you describe your proximity to the cross of Jesus? Give specific examples.

16. How near are you willing to be? What keeps you at a distance?

▶ READ JOHN 3:16; ROMANS 5:8; 8:35–39;
EPHESIANS 1:4–6; 2:4–5; 5:1–2, 25; 1 JOHN 3:16

17. How does knowing that God loves you encourage you to
draw near to the cross of Christ?

18. How does it help you to love others?

Commentary

Do you watch people? I enjoy watching people in various settings—athletic events, shopping malls, Christian conferences. Some are controllers. Some go unnoticed while others draw the attention of those passing by. Some are alone and make no eye contact with others; others are surrounded by peers and willing to talk to a stranger. Some people follow others wisely; others stumble along without thinking about the leader or the path. Some people are serious and intense; others are carefree. What about those who keep people at a safe distance? They are careful not to get too close to anyone, not to get too involved in anything. They keep themselves in a comfortable place, avoiding any risk or commitment. They "friend" many on Facebook but avoid real commitment. What kind of person are you?

All classes of people and individuals observed Jesus on the cross—Jew, Gentile, married, single, men, women, military, civilian, religious, nonreligious, politicians, family, friends, disciples, enemies. Regardless of what brought them there, they all witnessed the same event—a profound statement from God—but with different responses. The same cross both attracted and repelled. It was and is impossible to look at the cross and remain neutral or unchanged. Then and now, the cross demands a response from those who look at it. Some people, even unlikely people, respond with belief in Jesus Christ as the Redeemer. Others respond with rejection of Jesus as God's only way of salvation.

Four different groups of people watched Jesus' crucifixion: first, the crowd—passersby and Jewish religious leaders; second, centurions and other soldiers who were responsible to carry out the death sentence; third, two criminals crucified on either side of

Jesus; and finally, the followers of Jesus that included his mother, disciples, and friends—some nearby and some at a distance.

The Crowd (Matthew 27:39–43; Mark 15:29–32)

The Passersby

The people who passed by came from many different places along the main road where criminals were crucified. Some may have seen a crucifixion before. This one must have been quite a sight, considering the mob mentality of the crowd it drew. They threw insults at Jesus and mocked him. The sign on his cross identified him as the King of the Jews, but the people did not bother to investigate the truth of this designation. Instead, they "derided him, wagging their heads and saying, 'You who would destroy the temple and rebuild it in three days, save yourself! If you are the Son of God, come down from the cross'" (Matthew 27:39–40).

They questioned his very identity. They were like non-thinkers today who reject the claims of Jesus yet have not read the Bible for themselves. They criticize Christians who stand on the truth of the Bible, and they reject the Christ of the Bible without thinking through his claims, his works, and their eternal implications. They never analyze what they have heard, seen, or read. They do not care who Jesus Christ is or why he was crucified. They are simply too busy and comfortable with their lives to be bothered. After all, what could a dying man have to offer them? Some erroneously believe that Jesus died as a martyr or a victim, or that his death was useless. Others say it was cosmic child abuse if he really was the Son of God. How committed are you to study and think about what the Bible narrates and teaches? What are the consequences of your commitment?

The Jewish Religious Leaders

The Jewish religious leaders also mocked him, perhaps inciting the passersby to have the same mob mentality. With dripping sarcasm, they railed at him,

> He saved others; he cannot save himself. He is the King of Israel; let him come down now from the cross, and we will believe in him. He trusts in God; let God deliver him now, if he desires him. For he said, "I am the Son of God." (Matthew 27:42–43)

Their final taunt questioned his trust in his Father and his Father's love for him.

These leaders were thinkers, but their thinking was convoluted by their enjoyment of positions of power and influence. They did not want to lose their prestige and control over others. They realized that if Jesus' claims to be the Son of God were true, then he would legitimately have authority over their lives. They would be subject to him and his teaching, not to their own traditions or ideas. They foolishly decided that the best thing to do was to get rid of him, the one they mockingly identified as the Christ of God, the King of Israel, the King of the Jews, and God's Chosen One. These religious leaders found themselves against the very God they professed to worship. They demanded a miracle, but they had not believed the ones Jesus had already done. They had already rejected him, his words, and his works. Jesus never accommodated crowds who demanded a miracle before they would believe.

The religious leaders missed what they professed to be seeking and led others to do the same. Those who undermine the authority of the Bible, God's written Word, and the authority of Jesus Christ, God's living Word, reject the truth through negligence

(I'm too busy for this) or arrogance (I don't need this). Have you used these excuses, perhaps veiled in other terminology?

God demonstrated his authority over them at the cross through Pilate's refusal to change "Jesus of Nazareth, The King of the Jews" to "He claimed to be the King of the Jews." Anyone can make a claim. The sign correctly showed God's revelation of his Son. It was written in Aramaic, Latin, and Greek for each to read in his own language. Jesus demonstrated his authority over sin when he prayed for their forgiveness as he was nailed to the cross. He came down from the cross, but not in the way they expected. He died in order to be buried so that he could be resurrected—proof that he is the Son of God! In God's economy, death precedes life.

What do you learn from these people? They had hardened their hearts. They never stopped to ask, "What if he really is the Son of God?" If you do not examine the claims of Jesus, you may find yourself against him. If you refuse Jesus, you will find yourself against him. You cannot win against God. These people thought they had won, but they lost. For all eternity, they are recorded as being against their Creator. He will not relinquish his authority to another. The place of blessing is under the sovereign rule and authority of the Lord. True freedom is found at the cross of Jesus, looking up to him as the sovereign Lord of life.

The Centurions and Soldiers (Matthew 27:32–37, 54; Luke 23:33–38; John 19:17–24)

The second group of onlookers at Jesus' crucifixion included the centurions and soldiers. They did not understand the significance of their actions, as Jesus indicated in his prayer for their forgiveness (Luke 23:34). They were just doing their job, business as usual. They were used to carrying out executions by crucifixion. To them, Jesus was just another criminal being executed for doing wrong. They divided his clothes into four shares but did not want to tear the outer, seamless garment. They were unaware that dividing his outer garment by casting lots fulfilled Old Testament prophecy (Psalm 22:18). They were trying to get something for themselves without realizing that the man on the cross was the Lord of glory.

Jesus' crucifixion was not ordinary. Had anyone ever prayed for the soldiers' forgiveness? Those being executed probably cursed the soldiers as they were nailed to their crosses. This day, the soldiers also observed Jesus' promise of paradise to one of the criminals crucified with him. Later they heard the exchange between Jesus, Mary, and John. The last three hours that Jesus hung on the cross were divinely significant. Darkness covered the earth, as God hid his Son from view in the final hours of his substitutionary suffering for sin. In fact, the soldiers could see nothing. It was a penetrating kind of darkness.

What were they thinking during those three hours? Were they putting some of the pieces together and understanding something of the significance of the moment? Were they thinking about the words on the sign? They had to stay at their posts until the crucified were declared dead. Perhaps they slept. Perhaps they pondered Jesus' kingdom, which was not like the Roman empire. Their understanding may have been enhanced by the contrast between Jesus' crucifixion and others they had witnessed.

Suddenly at the end of the darkness, when Jesus died, the earth shook, the rocks split, the tombs were opened, and bodies of the dead were raised. The soldiers were filled with awe, proclaiming, "Truly this was the Son of God!" (Matthew 27:54). God mercifully intervened in their lives with extraordinary events to open their eyes to see the truth about Jesus Christ. The darkness and earthquake got their attention! They may not have understood much, but the light that shone in their minds and hearts was like a small candle in the midst of a completely dark room. God sometimes draws people to himself by turning their world upside down. He slows them down with crises, opening uninterested minds and closed hearts to examine the truth of his Son.

Are you like the soldiers, going about your business? Will God have to send an extraordinary event like unnatural darkness or an earthquake to get you to stop and think about Jesus and his claim to be the Son of God, the promised Messiah, and the Savior? Perhaps you are in the midst of a job loss, a family crisis, serious health concerns, disappointments personally or professionally, or false accusations with no opportunity to offer self-defense. Open your heart to the Savior on the cross, the Man of Sorrows who is acquainted with all kind of grief (Isaiah 53:3–4).

What can we learn from the centurions? Open-minded people are not those who believe everything they hear. Open-minded people weigh what they hear and see, rejecting what is not true and embracing what is true. Could God be working to cause you to look deeply at what he has done for you in Christ, to evaluate the evidence more closely and be convinced of it? To take your stand on the truth of Christ is to be on the only sure foundation.

Two Criminals (Luke 23:39–43)

Two criminals (Matthew calls them robbers) were crucified on either side of Jesus. Unlike Jesus, they were guilty and being justly punished. Initially, both railed at Jesus, mocking his claim to be the Christ and chiding him to save himself and them (Matthew 27:44; Mark 15:32). Later, one criminal turned to Jesus. The other blamed Jesus for not doing something to get him off the cross. In effect, he blamed God that he had been caught and sentenced to death, refusing to accept responsibility for his crime. He had no fear of the eternal consequences of his words. He was unwilling to acknowledge Jesus as the Christ.

The believing criminal rebuked the other for not fearing God. He acknowledged that he deserved his punishment and accepted responsibility for the sentence he received. He humbly asked Jesus to remember him when he came into his kingdom. How precious to hear Jesus' promise, "Today you will be with me in Paradise" (Luke 23:43), as the criminal's sins passed over onto Jesus.

What can we learn from these criminals? The truth of justification by grace alone through faith alone in Christ alone is clear in the criminal who trusted Jesus. He had no merit of his own to claim. There was no intermediate state either; he would be with Jesus in paradise that very day. We also learn that we will never get close to God as long as we blame him for the situations that we encounter through our sin. Yet even the most hopeless and least likely find mercy when they acknowledge their sin and cry out to God for forgiveness and mercy. Even Christians can fall into the trap of blaming God. We cannot lose eternal life, but we lose intimacy with God as our Father.

Does God seem far away today? Could it be that you are blaming him instead of taking responsibility for your actions and crying out to him for mercy? Believe 1 John 1:9 and be restored to him immediately. Conviction of sin is a gift of God's grace that leads to confession, repentance, and renewed fellowship with him. Do not give up; God's grace and mercy are new every morning (Lamentations 3:22–23). He is able to give you grace and mercy while remaining just, because Jesus took your punishment.

Jesus' Followers (Matthew 27:55–56; Mark 15:40–41; Luke 23:49; John 19:25–27)

At the Foot of the Cross

Some followers of Jesus stood at the foot of the cross; others watched from a distance. His mother and the disciple he loved were close enough to hear Jesus speak to them. In the midst of his intense suffering, Jesus' thoughts were toward others. His mother needed someone to care for her. Staying near the cross, Mary experienced Jesus' comforting words and John heard the privileged call to care for the mother of his Lord. The foot of the cross was the place to hear the Savior speak. Those who watched from afar had loved and cared for Jesus. Some apparently had been close to the cross but had moved to the edge at some point during the crucifixion. Nevertheless, they stayed within sight of the cross. Some of the women would follow him to his burial place.

Today

What keeps us from getting close to Jesus? First, we refuse to accept responsibility for ourselves—blaming others, circumstances, economy, disadvantages, and so on. Ultimately, we blame God (Genesis 3:12–13).

Second, we foolishly think that we can work to improve ourselves to rise above these circumstances. The Bible tells us that our biggest problem is our sin (inside us) and that God's solution is Christ (outside us). We cannot do enough to get close to God. Jesus is the only way to God.

Third, fear of what we might lose keeps us from receiving all that is ours in Christ. We fear being rejected by others. We fear that getting too close to Jesus will cost us our life. In fact, it will! To lose one's life for Christ is actually to find it (Matthew 16:25). However, Jesus promised that his presence would make our load easy and our burden light (Matthew 11:28–30).

Finally, we feel unworthy of the love that Christ demonstrated on the cross. How could God possibly love someone like me? Meditate on the following affirmations of God's love, demonstrated by Christ on the cross: John 3:16; Romans 5:8; 8:35–39; Ephesians 1:4–6; 2:4–5; 5:1–2; 1 John 3:16. Pondering Christ's cross assures us of God's love and stirs our hearts to love him. The more we understand God's love in Christ, the more we desire to cling to him and the more we cherish the unlimited access we have to his throne of grace.

What is your response as you look at Jesus' cross? Where will you take your stand? How near will you get? You cannot get to the place of greatest blessing unless you go through the cross and stay there. You either draw near to Jesus or move away. While watching these people, have you concluded that the place of greatest blessing is at the foot of his cross, looking to him and all that it cost him to die for you? Or are you one of the enthusiastic ones who go along with the crowd but then walk away, close the Bible, and give no more thought until next week?

Are you so busy with daily affairs that it may take an earthquake or an extended period of darkness to get you to stop and look at Jesus? If you do not heed his wooing voice, he may give you a wake-up call to get your attention. God interrupts our lives with stock market crashes, the unexpected departure of a loved one through death or desertion, the dreaded diagnosis of a life-threatening disease, natural disasters, and so on. These interruptions are opportunities to run to him. The world responded to 9/11 with increased church attendance, community prayer meetings, and religious talk. Sadly, most ran to God for a moment but quickly returned to their usual habits.

Do you fear losing control? "Being in control" is one of the most subtle lies of the world and the Devil. Everyone is under the control either of God or of those opposed to God. Your response to the cross reveals the condition of your heart.

> Carla moved closer to Jesus through looking at the people near the cross. "It's so easy to keep the cross at arm's length so as not to see the horror and suffering there and what it cost Jesus to pay the penalty for sin. As I studied the people at the cross, I began to see the cross as personal to me—Jesus' death for my sin, in my place. I couldn't hold it at arm's length any longer. I also discovered that the cross is a place of intimacy with my Savior, a place of security where I can hear his words of comfort and of deep love for me, his beloved child. Staying close to the cross is a place of great blessing. Focusing on the cross helps me to remember what Jesus did for me and to experience the comfort of his loving care. When tired, I find strength; when stressed, energy; amid struggles or confusion, peace and rest. When I am near the cross, my thinking is centered on Christ. The cross is where I understand my sin and God's love for me. Everything else fades as my priorities change; I am not so interested in money, popularity, or power. What matters more than anything else is to have the brightness of Jesus' face directed to me and to rejoice that I am his. Near the cross I can hear Jesus' words without distraction from the noisy world around me. My sin is covered with Jesus' blood. The sunshine of his

face brings a smile to mine as I am comforted by his loving care and by the challenge of his call on my life."

Do you know these blessings? If not, why are you not nearer to the cross? Read afresh the accounts of Jesus' last week in Matthew, Mark, Luke, and John. Take time to ponder the details and to thank God as you move slowly through the narrative. Write down the way that he blesses you and fills you with joyful anticipation of his loving care. It will be time well spent.

Closing Prayer

Lord God, my Father, help me to take my place as close to Jesus as I can be. May I cling to him and, like Mary, hear his comforting words and experience his loving care for me. Lord Jesus, as you did for John, entrust me with responsibility for other people. Help me to accept responsibility for my sin, confess it to you, and cry out for mercy. Enable me to forgive those who hurt me. Help me to say wholeheartedly, without reservation, "Lord Jesus, two wonders I confess: the wonders of your redeeming love and my unworthiness." Help me to turn to you as my abiding place, the place where I live moment by moment. May the world's pleasures and charms fade away in the light of seeing the sunshine of your face, my beautiful and wonderful Savior. In your precious and holy name. Amen. (Inspired by the hymn, "Beneath the Cross of Jesus")

The Words from the Cross

For out of the abundance of the heart the mouth speaks. The good person out of his good treasure brings forth good. (Matthew 12:34–35)

Texts

Matthew 27:32–50
Mark 15:22–37
Luke 23:32–43
John 19:16–30

Truth

Jesus' last words reveal his heart.

Hymn: "Jesus, Keep Me Near the Cross"

Jesus, keep me near the cross;
There a precious fountain,

Free to all—a healing stream—
Flows from Calv'ry's mountain.

Refrain:
In the cross, in the cross,
Be my glory ever;
Till my raptured soul shall find
Rest beyond the river.

Near the cross, a trembling soul,
Love and mercy found me;
There the Bright and Morning Star
Shed its beams around me. *Refrain*

Near the cross! O Lamb of God,
Bring its scenes before me;
Help me walk from day to day
With its shadow o'er me. *Refrain*

Near the cross I'll watch and wait,
Hoping, trusting ever,
Till I reach the golden strand
Just beyond the river. *Refrain*

—FANNY J. CROSBY, 1869

Opening Prayer

Holy God and Father, we are grateful to have the historical record of the cross. As are all stories in the Bible, we know it is true. Thank you that we are able to look in detail at the very words spoken by Jesus from the cross. Open our minds to understand, our hearts to embrace more deeply, and our lives to live out more fully the significance of these words for us. May we stay near the cross by remembering this story and reflecting on its blessing in our lives. Cleanse our hearts and fill them with truth, that our speech will be honoring to you and edifying to others. In the name of our Savior, Amen.

Questions for Study and Discussion

▶ READ MATTHEW 27:32–50; MARK 15:22–37; LUKE 23:32–43; JOHN 19:16–30

1. Try to discern and list the order of the recorded words of Jesus from the cross.

▶ READ LUKE 23:32–38

2. How did Jesus' words fulfill Old Testament prophecy and his own teaching?

    a. Isaiah 53:12

    b. Matthew 5:44

3. According to the following verses, who needed the forgiveness for which Jesus prayed?

a. Luke 23:33

b. Matthew 21:1–11 with Luke 23:21

c. 1 Corinthians 2:8 with Luke 23:34

d. Isaiah 53:4–6

▶ READ LUKE 23:39–43 WITH JOHN 5:24, 26;
 AND 6:37–40

4. How did Jesus continue proclaiming the kingdom of God
   in spite of his suffering?

5. What do you learn from Jesus about your responsibility to
   proclaim God's kingdom?

▶ **READ JOHN 19:26–27**

6. Using the following verses, explain how Jesus' words to Mary and John demonstrate the principles of the kingdom of God.

   a. Exodus 20:12

   b. Matthew 5:17

c. Mark 7:9–13

d. 1 Timothy 5:3

e. James 1:27

7. Give some examples of how you might honor your parents in light of these principles.

▶ READ MATTHEW 27:45–46; MARK 15:34; PSALM 22; ISAIAH 53:4–6; AND JOHN 1:29

8. What was the reason for the darkness from noon to 3 p.m.?

9. How might Psalm 22; Isaiah 53; and John 1:29 have been a comfort to Jesus?

▶ READ JOHN 19:28–29

10. Using the following verses, explain the significance of his words "I thirst."

a. Psalm 69:21

b. Psalm 22:14–15

c. John 4:10, 13–14

▶ READ JOHN 19:30 AND ISAIAH 53:11–12

11. What was finished?

12. How do Jesus' words reveal his joyous expectation after the long hours of agony?

13. What encourages you about "It is finished"?

▶ READ JOHN 19:30 WITH MATTHEW 27:50;
MARK 15:37; LUKE 23:46; AND JOHN 10:17–18

14. Is it possible for us to dismiss our spirits in this way? Explain, using Acts 7:59–60.

15. What hope and joy have you received from studying Jesus' words from the cross?

16. With whom might you share this hope and joy?

Commentary

Sometimes I look at my husband and think, "I know just what he is thinking." A few minutes later I am surprised at what he has just said. How could I miss what is so important to him? How can you tell what is important to another person? Listen to what the person says.

Jesus said, "Out of the abundance of the heart his mouth speaks" (Luke 6:45). We talk about what we most treasure or value. Jesus' words from the cross were few, but they revealed what was most important to him. His mind was filled with the Scripture and with God's purpose in sending him to earth. His heart reached out to those around him.

Remember the overarching narrative of the Bible: God is redeeming a people for himself. He sent Jesus to be the Redeemer. Jesus would pay the ransom for those God had given him. They would be in him when he returned to heaven in his preincarnate glory. Jesus, the Son of God, became a man and proclaimed the kingdom of God and himself as its King. While on earth, he taught and demonstrated what the kingdom of God is like. On the cross, he continued his prayers and his practice as King, demonstrating and teaching life in the kingdom of God—forgiving, caring, calling, and giving life. He continued calling those whom the Father had given him.

The Gospels record seven statements Jesus made as he was crucified. He was not absorbed with his pain or suffering; his focus was on his mission and the people he came to save. The first three statements were directed to people at the cross as he reached out to them with the message of forgiveness, eternal life, and compassion. The last four fulfilled Old Testament prophecies. Jesus' thoughts on the promises and prophecies of God kept the joy before him as he endured the suffering.

"Father, Forgive Them, for They Know Not What They Do" (Luke 23:32–38)

As Jesus was nailed to the cross, he prayed for those crucifying him, fulfilling the prophecy of Isaiah 53:12. Jesus also demonstrated his own teaching, "Love your enemies and pray for those who persecute you" (Matthew 5:44). The Roman soldiers were doing business as usual. They did not know that the one they were nailing to the cross was the Son of God, the promised Messiah. They were unaware of the enormity of their actions against him and the significance of them in God's plan of redemption. His death provided what the soldiers needed to be forgiven. When the cross was in place, the soldiers "cast lots to divide his garments" (Luke 23:34). Jesus must have remembered the prophecy of Psalm 22:18.

Who needed the forgiveness for which Jesus prayed? Who actually crucified Jesus? Was it only the soldiers? Did it include the Jewish leaders? They had more understanding of who Jesus was. They had purposely sidestepped the law in the trials of Jesus. What about the others at the scene? The people had heard his teaching and witnessed his mighty works. They had hailed him as the Son of David (Messiah), who came in the name of the Lord, just a few days earlier (Matthew 21:1–11). Now they repeatedly shouted, "Crucify him!" (Luke 23:21). They did not understand all they were doing, or they would not have crucified him (1 Corinthians 2:8). Likewise, every sinner bears responsibility for Jesus' death (Romans 3:10–11). Everyone who receives him as Savior and Lord is an answer to this prayer for his Father's forgiveness. Are you?

"Truly, I Say to You, Today You Will Be with Me in Paradise" (Luke 23:39–43)

Two criminals were crucified, one on either side of Jesus. Both joined the mockers, railing against him, "Are you not the Christ? Save yourself and us!" One later confessed his sin and the just punishment for it. And he said, "Jesus, remember me when you come into your kingdom." Jesus replied, "Truly, I say to you, today you will be with me in Paradise." This exchange of words may have been early in the hours Jesus spent on the cross. Certainly, it was before the sixth hour (noon) when darkness covered the land (Matthew 27:45). Again Jesus demonstrated his authority to give life and his power to call the citizens of his kingdom. One criminal was assured of forgiveness and eternity with Jesus through faith; the other died refusing the revelation of Jesus' majesty and compassion on the cross.

How encouraging to see that it is never too late and that no one is too bad to receive God's grace and forgiveness. Grandpa, ninety years old, did not want to hear anything about Jesus. His only grandson and namesake, James, cried as a boy, "Grandpa doesn't know Jesus!"

As Grandpa neared the end of his life, James, who was now married and serving his country in the U.S. Navy, still cried about Grandpa's eternal destiny. He traveled across the country to see him, praying that he would not be too late. He arrived when Grandpa was asleep. Praying for wisdom and courage, he lightly touched Grandpa's shoulder. Opening his eyes, Grandpa recognized James and was lucid enough to converse. The conversation went like this. "Grandpa, there is something very important to me. May I tell you about it?"

"Sure."

"When I die, I know I'm going to heaven to be with Jesus. It's very important to me that you will be there too. May I talk to you about that?"

"Sure."

As James respectfully presented the gospel through a series of questions, Grandpa acknowledged his sin and expressed faith in Jesus as his Savior. James said, "You can tell God what you just told me. Would you like me to help you?"

"Yes." Grandpa prayed phrase by phrase as James led him. James paused several times to make sure he used the correct words. Grandpa kept praying, and he said the right words! James left knowing that he would never see Grandpa again on earth but confident that he would see him in heaven. The Holy Spirit had given Grandpa life and faith to believe, even to articulate his beliefs without James's help. Years of family prayers were answered as God adopted Grandpa into his family. When questioned later, James acknowledged that he was a man with a mission. "This was too important to ignore."

"Woman, Behold, Your Son! . . . Behold, Your Mother!" (John 19:26–27)

It is not certain whether these words were spoken before or after the words to the criminal. Traditionally, the church has put them after. At some point after the soldiers divided his clothes, Jesus saw his mother and John the apostle standing nearby. Mary was probably a widow, since Joseph is not mentioned in Jesus' adult ministry.

Jesus knew his obligation to care for his mother personally and financially. One of the Ten Commandments explicitly stated, "Honor your father and your mother" (Exodus 20:12). He honored her by being more concerned for her care than for his comfort. Jesus again demonstrated what he taught, "Do not think that I have come to abolish the Law or the Prophets; I have not come to abolish them but to fulfill them" (Matthew 5:17). He had rebuked the Pharisees for circumventing this very commandment (Mark 7:9–13). Later, Paul wrote, "Honor widows who are truly widows" (1 Timothy 5:3) and James recorded, "Religion that is pure and undefiled before God, the Father, is this: to visit orphans and widows in their affliction, and to keep oneself unstained from the world" (James 1:27).

How does your life honor your parents and reach out to widows in affliction? My parents are both in heaven; because of this commandment, I have committed to say nothing that would dishonor them. I choose to remember and recite their honorable traits and acts of kindness.

Jesus blessed John with additional responsibility. Our King does the same today for those who faithfully serve him and are close enough to listen to him. Jesus taught and demonstrated this important kingdom principle: the reward for faithfulness is greater responsibility (Matthew 25:29).

What is your response to greater responsibility in God's kingdom? The more you love Christ, the more he will ask of you. While additional responsibility may seem a burden, it is actually a blessing from the Savior. What might you do to teach and demonstrate the joy of serving in God's kingdom?

"My God, My God, Why Have You Forsaken Me?" (Matthew 27:46; Psalm 22:1)

To individuals nearby, Jesus' work from the cross appeared complete. Now from the sixth hour (noon) there was darkness over all the land until the ninth hour (3 p.m.). This darkness looked back to the "darkness to be felt" of the plague on Egypt (Exodus 10:21). We get some sense of it when we descend into a cave. The guide turns off the light and tells us to look at our hands in front of our faces, but we cannot see them. Darkness was associated with God's judgment and death. This supernatural darkness covered all the land, a statement of God's righteous anger against humanity for their sin in crucifying his Son.

Silence from the cross accentuated the darkness. The wrath of God poured out on Jesus was between him and his Father-God. No one was allowed to observe it. "The darkness veiled the anguish of the Son of God while he was bearing the punishment for our sins, because it was not right for human eyes to look on him in his suffering. At the same time, the darkness cried out against the blackness of our sin and testified to the tremendous cost to God of our redemption."[1] We do not know Jesus' thoughts, but we know he understood how all the Old Testament was about him (Luke 24:44–47). He

1. James Montgomery Boice, *The Gospel of Matthew*, vol. 2 (Grand Rapids, MI: Baker, 2001), 623.

knew the Old Testament prophecies of his sacrificial death. He was living out Psalm 22 and Isaiah 52:13–53:12.

The darkness may also have been God's mercy for those nearby. Isaiah had foretold, "His appearance was so marred, beyond human semblance, and his form beyond that of the children of mankind" (Isaiah 52:14). If that described the effects of his physical abuse, who could bear the sight of God's wrath poured out on him as he was made sin (2 Corinthians 5:21) and became a curse (Galatians 3:13)? More horrible than our minds can conceive or our words can describe is what he bore for the joy of redeeming those whom the Father had given him.

For three silent hours, Jesus did not just feel forsaken; he was forsaken. Intimacy with his Father was broken. He was abandoned, separated from the presence of his holy Father, an offering for sin and guilt, "stricken, smitten by God . . . afflicted . . . pierced . . . crushed . . . the LORD has laid on him the iniquity of us all" (Isaiah 53:4–6). Suddenly, at about the ninth hour, Jesus broke the silence, crying out with a loud voice, "My God, my God, why have you forsaken me?" There was no answer, for he had been experiencing the horrors of hell, separation from his Father and abandonment by his God. There will be no comfort from God for those who are under his eternal wrath. Nevertheless, God heard Jesus' cry! "For he has not despised or abhorred the affliction of the afflicted, and he has not hidden his face from him, but has heard, when he cried to him" (Psalm 22:24).

He was not forsaken forever. The ransom had been paid; our debt was canceled. He, the Lamb of God, had taken away our sin and guilt (John 1:29). We will not be forsaken because he was forsaken in our place. He will present us to his Father in glory!

"I Thirst" (John 19:28)

Jesus had refused a sedative drink on the way to the cross (Matthew 27:34; Mark 15:23). He had to bear the full wrath of God for our sins; there could be no minimizing the pain. He had to be alert to the needs of those around him, the King demonstrating life in the kingdom and granting forgiveness, life, and care. He had to fulfill every prophecy of the cross. Now Jesus knew his work was finished (John 19:28). His words, "I thirst," fulfilled Psalm 69:21. Was this physical thirst or something more? Did his parched throat and tongue need moisture to speak the remaining words from the cross? Dehydration was part of crucifixion, depleting the body. At some point, his entire body would burn because of it. However, his thirst was more than physical.

Thirst is also used in the Scripture for deep, inward spiritual emptiness that can be satisfied only by God himself (Psalm 22:10–11, 19). Hell, the place of eternal wrath, is the place where there is no one to bring relief. Jesus told a parable about the rich man in hell with no one to bring him water (Luke 16:24). People foolishly say, "I'll take my chances in hell!" or "I'll join my pals in hell and we'll have a big party." But there is no water there, no respite, no satisfaction, and no end to the thirst of your soul. Neither is there any Facebook or community. Jesus had living water to give to others but could not drink it himself while on the cross (John 4:10, 13–14) or his mission would have been aborted.

What is your deepest need? For what do you thirst? To whom or what do you go to find satisfaction for it? A friend? A box of chocolate? A cup of coffee? A glass of wine? Your river cottage or lakefront property? Surfing? Anything to distract your thoughts of thirst? Only Jesus can satisfy your real need for God. He is the only one who is perfect and able to satisfy your soul. The cross is the place where you can run for the satisfaction that he alone gives.

"It Is Finished" (John 19:30; Psalm 22:31)

Jesus had finished his work and was ready to proclaim his victory. This was no whimper or gasp. With a shout, he exclaimed, "It is finished!" What was finished? He had completed his earthly life and mission, the work the Father sent him to accomplish. His words revealed what was in his heart. He had proclaimed the kingdom and shown himself to be its King by his words and works. He had offered himself as the sin offering to provide forgiveness and removal of guilt to make the kingdom's citizens acceptable. The ransom was paid in full. The wrath of God was satisfied. There is no more need for Jesus to die again or for his people to pay for their sins or carry the load of their guilt. He redeemed a people for the Father and himself. He paid the price for his bride and is now preparing to take her home to heaven to be with him forever, glorified and like him.

Are you prepared for the wedding celebration in heaven through faith in Jesus' finished work for you? If you have received Jesus Christ as your Savior, you will never be separated from God. You will eternally enjoy intimate fellowship with the Father, the Son, and the Holy Spirit. God's face will be turned toward you forever, because it was turned away from Christ in your place on the cross. You will be clothed in Christ's perfect righteousness—a bride to behold.

"Father, into Your Hands I Commit My Spirit" (Luke 23:46)

Jesus' final breath was not the result of crucifixion although he was exhausted, dehydrated, and suffering blood loss, shock, fatigue, and suffocation. No one took his life. His last breath was his final deliberate act. He had told his disciples earlier,

> For this reason the Father loves me, because I lay down my life that I may take it up again. No one takes it from me, but I lay it down of my own accord. I have authority to lay it down, and I have authority to take it up again. This charge I have received from my Father. (John 10:17–18)

This time he spoke to God as "Father," rather than "God," quoting Psalm 31:5. Again with a loud voice, Jesus said, "Father, into your hands I commit my spirit" (Luke 23:46). "He bowed his head and gave up his spirit" (John 19:30). This was his human spirit, not the Holy Spirit.[2]

Is it possible for us to dismiss our spirits in this way? We do not have the same authority over life and death that Jesus had. People may take their lives by suicide, but that is different from what Jesus did. However, his example helps us to face death and the process of dying, just as it helped Stephen and other Christian martyrs. Stephen cried out, "Lord Jesus, receive my spirit" and "Lord, do not hold this sin against them" as he was being stoned (Acts 7:59–60).

When you face death, like my friend Tom, you can quote Scripture and follow Jesus' example of thinking of the joy that awaits you as you pass from this life into eternity with him. Through memorization, you can deliberately remember and consciously cling to the promises and prophecies of Scripture that speak of your redemption and glory with

2. Taken from study note on John 19:30 in the *ESV® Study Bible* (The Holy Bible, *English Standard Version®*), copyright 2008 by Crossway, a publishing ministry of Good News Publishers.

Jesus. By his power, his Spirit, and his Word, you can live by the Scripture, committing yourself daily into your Father's hands. This prepares you for death.

I have asked my family not to talk about weather, politics, or "stuff" if I linger. I want them to read the Bible to me, talk about the hope of heaven, and remind me of God's promises, the assurance that I am God's adopted child, Jesus' prayer in John 17, the cross and its demonstration of how to die, and so on. I want them to sing, read, or play my favorite hymns. I want them to worship Jesus with me and pray with me. If I am unable to respond, I want them to do these things anyway. Perhaps I will be able to hear even though I cannot respond. We can do this for others for whom death is imminent. I had the privilege of reading the psalms to my dying aunt and of singing "Lift High the Cross" as my older sister took her last breath. I was near the cross in each of those moments.

Those near the cross heard Jesus speak. How do we stay close to the cross? We read and sing about it, remembering its significance. How does he speak to us? He speaks through the Bible. We study the Bible to know it, live it, and saturate ourselves in its promises. That is why we have looked at the big picture of the cross and then looked closely at different facets of it. By faith, we commit ourselves into Jesus' hands step by step. Then we will be ready to yield to him when he calls us home.

Where do you turn for comfort, strength, hope, forgiveness, and peace? Look at the words of Jesus. Jesus keeps us near the cross for cleansing, mercy, love, and a look at the brightness of our Savior. We can review his sacrificial death. We can see him as the source of hope, trust, and focus beyond the present to the end of our story. Our story ends with glory in the presence of Christ. We will be forever free from the presence of sin in us, and we will be in the sin-free new heaven and earth. Is that your story? If you are in Christ, it is.

Closing Prayer

Lord Jesus, thank you that your words reveal your heart on the cross. Help me to remember who you are, what you did there, and what you said there. Give me understanding that your sacrificial death finished God's requirement for my atonement. Help me to learn what it means to be near the cross and to rejoice in all you have finished for me in my place and on my behalf. When it is time for me to join you in heaven, keep me focused on your kingdom and glory. In your mighty, powerful, and precious name. Amen.

The Power of the Cross

And what is the immeasurable greatness of his power toward us who believe, according to the working of his great might that he worked in Christ when he raised him from the dead and seated him at his right hand in the heavenly places. . . . Now to him who is able to do far more abundantly than all that we ask or think, according to the power at work within us, to him be glory in the church and in Christ Jesus throughout all generations, forever and ever. Amen. (Ephesians 1:19–20; 3:20–21)

Texts

Matthew 27:51–66
Mark 15:38–47
Luke 23:44–56
John 19:31–42
2 Timothy 1:12
2 Timothy 2:11–13
Hebrews 4:16

Hebrews 7:25
Hebrews 10:19–25
Revelation 21

Truth

Jesus died on the cross that we might be free to love, obey, and serve God.

Hymn: "Turn Your Eyes upon Jesus"

O soul, are you weary and troubled?
No light in the darkness you see?
There's light for a look at the Savior,
And life more abundant and free!

Refrain
Turn your eyes upon Jesus,
Look full in his wonderful face;
And the things of earth will grow strangely dim
In the light of his glory and grace.

Through death into life everlasting
He passed and we follow him there;
Over us sin no more hath dominion—
For more than conqu'rors we are! *Refrain*

His Word shall not fail you—he promised;
Believe him and all will be well;
Then go to a world that is dying,
His perfect salvation to tell! *Refrain*

—HELEN HOWARTH LEMMEL, 1922

Opening Prayer

Faithful God, how grateful we are for the Lord Jesus Christ, our Savior from sin. From death into life everlasting he has passed, and we will follow him there. Your Word will never fail us. So we turn our eyes upon Jesus as we are weary and often troubled, seeing no light in the darkness of our circumstances and relationships. May our look at Jesus open our eyes to see the free and abundant life that he gives. May we wholeheartedly believe what you have promised, and then tell others of his perfect, free salvation from the penalty of sin, from the power of sin, and ultimately from the presence of sin. For the glory of our gracious Savior. Amen.

Questions for Study and Discussion

▶ READ MATTHEW 27:51–66; MARK 15:38–47; LUKE 23:44–56; JOHN 19:31–42

God exerted his power in the cross and the events accompanying it.

1. What miraculous events happened when Jesus died?

2. Was Jesus really physically dead? Why is this important? Explain your answer.

3. How did Jesus' death and burial fulfill Scripture?

4. Why are the recorded facts about Jesus' burial important? (See also Romans 6:4.)

5. Why do we bury dead bodies? How is this related to sin in the Christian's life?

6. What do you need to bury by Christ's power?

▶ READ HEBREWS 4:16; 7:25; 10:19–39

Jesus died to empower us to live for God in the present.

7. How are Hebrews 4:16 and 10:19–21 related to Matthew 27:51?

8. How have you approached God with confidence to receive mercy and find grace in your times of need this week?

9. How does knowing that Jesus is your High Priest help you?

10. Explain the attitudes you need in order to draw near to God (Hebrews 10:22–23, 35–39). How will you implement them?

11. What are you doing to stir up others to love and good works, especially by meeting together (Hebrews 10:24–25)?

12. What has Jesus given you to help you live for him? See John 16:7, 13–15; 17:17; and Galatians 5:22–23.

13. How are you using his help?

► READ 2 TIMOTHY 1:12; 2:11–13; 4:18;
AND REVELATION 21

Jesus died so that we can face the future.

14. What about the future frightens you?

15. How does Jesus' faith in God's promises to him show you how to face certain death and the uncertainties of the future without fear?

16. Which promises to God's people encourage you to face the future without fear? Use any verses from this lesson, or use others that you know.

17. Write a prayer of thanksgiving for the hope that God has given you from the truths in this lesson.

"If only I . . . what if I . . . ?" Memories linger and impede our growth in Christ. Sin entangles us. We feel trapped and helpless. What robs you of joy? What do you fear about the future? Is there an answer to the tyranny of the past, present, and future? Yes! At the cross, the Lord Jesus Christ defeated Satan, sin, and death—enemies that enslave us and grip us with fear. We are no longer in their camp; we have been transferred through faith in Christ "to the kingdom of [God's] beloved Son" (Colossians 1:13).

The religious leaders, Roman officials, crowds, and passersby railed at Jesus with scorn, derision, bitterness, and hatred. At last he was dying and finished. It seemed the Devil and those he influenced had won in bringing the Son of God to the cross. But Jesus defeated Satan and guaranteed his ultimate doom through what appeared to be Satan's greatest victory (Genesis 3:15). Jesus' death was the atoning sacrifice that God required for the forgiveness of sin. His enemies actually accomplished God's plan by crucifying Jesus. "He disarmed the rulers and authorities and put them to open shame, by triumphing over them in him" (Colossians 2:15).

Jesus' body was buried. The religious leaders did everything possible to keep his dead body in the tomb (Matthew 27:62–66). But nothing and no one could keep him there. Jesus' death, burial, and resurrection displayed God's power through miraculous signs. That same power enables believers to love and serve God unencumbered by the past, present, or future.

Signs of the Death of Jesus

God displayed his sovereign power over the miraculous events of Jesus' death. Several signs confirmed that Jesus physically died as the Old Testament foretold.

Blood and Water (John 19:31–37)

The first sign was the blood and water flowing from Jesus' pierced side. The executioners broke the legs of a crucified person to keep him from pushing up his body, hastening death by asphyxiation. These seasoned executioners had heard Jesus give up his spirit and could tell he was already dead. He, the Lamb of God who takes away the sin of the world, fulfilled the requirement that the bones of the Passover Lamb not be broken (Exodus 12:46; John 1:29). The soldiers pierced his side as prophesied (Zechariah 12:10). The mixture of blood and water that flowed was proof he was dead. Jesus' death was according to God's plan, not to man's usual procedures for crucifixion.

The Torn Curtain (Matthew 27:51)

The second sign was the tearing of the temple curtain. The temple was in the center of several courtyards. A veil separated the courtyards from the Holy Place, where the priests did their duties. A thicker curtain separating the Holy Place from the Most Holy Place was accessible only by the high priest on the Day of Atonement. To go beyond this curtain meant death. It "was an elaborately woven fabric of 72 twisted plaits of 24 threads each. It was 60 feet (18 m) high and 30 feet (9.1 m) wide."[1] It would not be easily torn, yet it was torn from top to bottom at three o'clock in the afternoon, the end of the darkness and the beginning of the evening sacrifice. "The priests would have been in the temple, engaged in their duties, when the veil was

1. Taken from study note on Matthew 27:51 in the *ESV® Study Bible* (The Holy Bible, *English Standard Version®*), copyright 2008 by Crossway, a publishing ministry of Good News Publishers.

torn."[2] Imagine their thoughts as it was torn from top to bottom, something only God could do. They suddenly had unrestricted access into the Most Holy Place. What if their eyes beheld God's presence and they were struck dead?

The miracle of the torn curtain has great spiritual significance (Hebrews 9:11–10:22). God opened the way to his presence by the death of his Son. No more would anyone need to offer animal sacrifices daily or annually on the Day of Atonement. God accepted Jesus, the perfect, final sacrifice. Nothing more can or must be done to reconcile sinners to God. Believers now have direct access to God.[3]

The Earthquake (Matthew 27:51–53)

The third sign was the earthquake. The miracle is not the earthquake but its timing at the exact moment of Jesus' death. With it, the rocks split, tombs were opened, and bodies of saints were raised and appeared in the city after Jesus was resurrected. The Bible does not explain who the saints were, how long they were resurrected, what they said, or to whom they appeared. Nevertheless, they point to Jesus' promise, "I am the resurrection and the life. Whoever believes in me, though he die, yet shall he live, and everyone who lives and believes in me shall never die" (John 11:25–26). Sin was judged, its guilt was removed, and death was defeated.

Soldiers' Faith (Matthew 27:54; Mark 15:39)

The fourth sign was the faith of the centurion and of those with him. Looking at Jesus on the cross and faced with the evi-

2. James Montgomery Boice, *The Gospel of Matthew*, vol. 2 (Grand Rapids, MI: Baker, 2001), 624.

3. See ibid., 624–26, for further explanation.

dence of Jesus' person and death, these soldiers confessed the truth that he is the Son of God.

Jesus' Burial (Matthew 27:57–61; Isaiah 53:9)

The fifth sign was the burial of Jesus exactly as God had foretold. He was tenderly buried in the unused tomb of wealthy Joseph of Arimathea. The leaders ordered that the tomb be sealed with a stone to prevent removal of his body. Mary Magdalene and other women witnessed the burial. These facts would rebut the foolish theories denying his death and resurrection that would be propagated through the ages. Jesus really died. His burial and resurrection removed the dread of the grave for his people.

Visible signs confirmed the plan and power of God. Historical records confirm Jesus' death and burial. Our faith is not based on some mystical experience of one person on a mountaintop. Christianity is based on eyewitnesses and on observable and verifiable facts.

Power for Believers

The cross was the path to Jesus' resurrection. The same power that raised Jesus from the dead enables Jesus' followers to overcome the past that hinders and entangles, to live joyfully in the present, and to face the future without fear or doubt.

Power to Overcome the Past

Jesus died to heal our grief, forgive our sin, and remove our guilt. What waves of past grief, shame, and pain roll over you—death, darkness, despair, desertion? He is your hope in these times. Is your heart breaking? He is the comfort and strength you need to pick up your bed of sorrow and walk in faith (Matthew 9:6).

Jesus bore your grief and sorrow that you might not have to live in the pain of the past.

What guilt plagues you? Do you feel guilty because you fell short of your expectations? Do you continue to agonize over denying Jesus through silence or deserting him through fear? Are you having trouble forgiving yourself? Beware of putting yourself above God, who has forgiven you. Playing "if only; what if" is a waste of time; you cannot rewrite history. Trying to do so keeps you enslaved to your past and its consequences.

> It is not just sinners who carry guilt. Innocent victims of abuse more often than not suffer from unbridled shame and false guilt. Abusers keenly manipulate their victims into thinking that they are responsible for the abuse inflicted on them. This can carry a lifelong sentence of fear, rejection, and unworthiness. Karen confided, "Nothing eradicated this malevolent lingering condition. Decades of therapy and analytical research left me still carrying my ponderously heavy sense of shame. When I learned that Jesus' death and burial are my death to this sin of another and my burial of the resulting shame, things changed. Daily I am tempted to go back, but as I remember Jesus' victory and seek God's strength, my shame is being replaced with the assurance of God's divine love. Moment by moment, I remind myself of this great wonder."

Jesus' death and burial are your death to sin and burial of it (Romans 6:1–4). Every weight and sin that clings so closely to you was buried with Jesus. Jesus' victory on the cross gives his people strength when they are tempted and tried and when they sometimes fail. He gives us power to live without the weight of guilt and to break the power of sin and of the flesh. Paul explains that believers are united with Christ in his death and burial that we may walk in newness of life.

A dead person's body is buried or burned because it is no longer in the sphere of this life. Likewise, your sin and guilt, buried with Christ in his death, are no longer part of your life. They are out of sight because you have a different focus and power. Clinging to your past when you are united to Christ is like exhuming a dead body.

What sin or shame enslaves you today? Do you have a recurring sinful habit of your tongue, lips, eyes, ears, mind, hands, or feet? Are you ashamed of what another did to you? Do you doubt God's promises? Are you afraid to get too close to Jesus? Identify your specific sins. Admit that they are heavy and are so much a part of you that you cannot in your own strength remove them.

Have a burial today. Write the pain, sorrow, guilt, sin, or shame on a piece of paper; picture the paper and its contents nailed to Christ, who carried them to the cross. By faith, lay them in Jesus' tomb and ask God to help you to leave them out of sight and to move forward by his power. Burn the paper so that you cannot exhume the "dead body."

Power to Live for God in the Present

Because your sin and guilt are buried with Christ, you can look to the risen Jesus each moment, drawing his strength and power to live for God in the present. Look beyond yourself to stir up other Christians to love and good works (Hebrews 10:24).

Jesus' death provided access to God (Hebrews 10:19–23). How precious it is to draw near to God with confidence. You may come to God boldly because of his marvelous grace, humbly because

215

of who you once were, and confidently because of what Christ did for you. Come with a true heart, in full assurance of faith in his finished work on the cross, and with a clear conscience. Come without wavering; his promises are true, for he is faithful (Hebrews 10:23).

Jesus' death guaranteed his resurrection and ascension (Philippians 2:8–11). Because Jesus died on the cross, God highly exalted him, giving him the name above every name. God, not you or any other person, "has made him both Lord and Christ" (Acts 2:36). God gave him all authority in heaven and on earth (Matthew 28:18). All will someday bow before him, agreeing with the Father that Jesus is Lord. Christians look to him as Lord in every area of life—serving him, trusting his prayers as our great High Priest, and pressing on to our high calling (Philippians 3:12–17). Instead of chafing at the idea of someone having authority over us, we find peace and safety in entrusting our lives into the hands of our Creator, Redeemer, and Lord.

Jesus' death resulted in the Spirit's indwelling and empowering (John 16:7, 13–15). We are not alone in living for God. The Holy Spirit lives within all who trust Jesus as Savior and who honor him as Lord. For the joy of heaven in Christ and by the power of the Spirit, we face the challenges of life in a sinful world whose values clash with God's Word. The Spirit assures us that we are God's children and heirs with Christ, provided that we suffer with him (Romans 8:14–17). How can we embrace the challenges of being a Christian? We believe God. We trust that God will do what he promised. Do you? The result will be that we are also glorified with Jesus. The joyful anticipation of that day enables us to follow Jesus' example of endurance (Hebrews 12:2).

Power to Face the Future

The miraculous signs from God at Jesus' death were preparatory to the greatest sign—the resurrection. God showed his acceptance of Jesus' sacrifice by raising him from the dead. We can face the future because he has gone before us in life and in death. He ascended into heaven and now rules from God's right hand.

Jesus' resurrection gives us hope to trust God with tomorrow's unknowns. We are not promised a life of ease and comfort. In fact, Christians are promised suffering as preparation for glory. What can we do when we hear distressing news of potentially terminal illness, miscarriage, divorce, or terrorism? What is our hope for our nation and the world? How do we cope with choices our children make today that point to deep sorrow or suffering for them and us tomorrow? Jesus is the answer to these questions. We pour out our concerns to him who is trustworthy and who completely understands what we need.

Jesus' resurrection enables us to face death without fear. Do you fear death? What is the basis for your fear? Is it that you do not know the promises of God for his people? Or do you doubt that God will keep them for you? God promises a new heaven and a new earth, where there will be no more tears, death, mourning, crying, pain, or regrets. Nothing accursed will be there, but our Triune God—Father, Son, and Holy Spirit—will be present and reigning. We will join the multitudes worshiping them (Revelation 22:1–5). When fearful of death, we look to the hope of heaven and of Jesus, who is waiting there for us (John 14:1–6).

Do you fear the process of dying? Sometimes the process is long, painful, and horrendous. God promises to be with you

(Hebrews 13:5). Jesus has experienced the death process, so he understands all that you may face. Come to him and be strengthened (Matthew 11:28–30).

> For two months, I walked through the valley of the shadow of death with my daughter's piano teacher. J. K. had two malignant brain tumors. There was no time for idle chatter. Death was imminent. God graciously led our conversation one evening, lifting her thoughts to the presence of God as I asked, "Are you afraid to die?"
>
> "Yes." Remembering the gospel and hearing about heaven, she affirmed her belief in Jesus Christ as her Lord and Savior.
>
> "Are you afraid to live?"
>
> "Yes." The assurance that God is always present with his people transformed her anxiety into peace. A few minutes later, her doctor called to say that she should return to the hospital. Throughout the forty-minute trip, she spoke constantly about how wonderful heaven would be and how glad she was to be going there. She entered the Lord's presence one month later, anticipating heaven and the joy of being with Jesus as his bride and seeing him in all his glory. She never wavered through unbelief. God's grace was sufficient for whatever happened.

Are you facing or grieving the death of a loved one? Do you fear going on living? God, the Father of our Lord Jesus, is the Father of mercies and the God of all comfort (2 Corinthians 1:3–4). He will comfort you and enable you to grieve properly, then to move forward, trusting his love and power to care for you.

Do you fear judgment? If you have received Jesus as your Savior, God's judgment for your sin was finished at the cross. You need not fear God's holy and just wrath. Jesus took your sins on himself and removed your guilt when he died. He bore God's wrath in your place and on your behalf. He will be waiting for you with open arms. Read Isaiah 52:13–53:12 when doubts assail you. If you are trusting another way to be saved, carefully read John's gospel. Ask God to show you the truth about Jesus and to give you faith to believe and have life in his name.

Do you fear that you will not make it to the finish line? Marathons are long and hard. Christians run a lifetime marathon against the culture whose worldview despises God and biblical truth. It seems that we are always swimming upstream against the current. What is the answer to the struggle? Paul wrote, "One thing I do: forgetting what lies behind and straining forward to what lies ahead, I press on toward the goal for the prize of the upward call of God in Christ Jesus" (Philippians 3:13–14). Your glory is the prize that Jesus asked God to give him in John 17. You will be forever with Jesus and the Father, free from sin, seeing Jesus as he is. You need not fear falling away through your failure, for God will empower you to run the race to the finish line. He will finish what he began in you (Philippians 1:6; 2:13). Will you speak God's words when tempted to fear? God has promised that you will be with Jesus forever. Rest on his promises (1 John 3:1–3).

We stand forgiven at the cross. Sin, guilt, and death are defeated foes. We move forward to love and serve God in the power of Christ's completed atoning sacrifice, resurrection, ascension, and reign. Whatever comes, God has already demonstrated that he cares by his love manifested in the cross of Christ. He has also demonstrated that he can help us by the power of the cross. "The Power of the Cross" by Keith Getty, sung by Kristyn Getty, beautifully gives this message.[4]

4. Kristyn Getty, "The Power of the Cross," by Keith Getty and Stuart Townend, on *New Irish Hymns #4: Hymns for the Life of the Church*, Kingsway Publications, 2005, compact disc. Uploaded online by the Gettys at https://www.youtube.com/watch?v=_ms-gxEOtLA.

God cares and God can! Let us live as though we believe that, running with confidence to the cross and the resurrection of our Savior to find power to overcome our past, power to live joyfully in the present, and power to face the future with confidence in our great God. Will you turn your eyes upon Jesus?

Closing Prayer

Thank you, my Father, that you care and that you can. You demonstrated your love for me in the cross of Christ. Your power was manifested in the power of his atoning sacrifice and resurrection. Help me to live in light of your loving care and mighty power given to me in Christ. May I believe that you are able to empower me to overcome my past, live joyfully in the present, and face the future with confidence in you. Help me to run to the cross and the empty tomb. May I use the freedom that Christ bought for me to love and serve you, my great God and Father. In the mighty name of Jesus. Amen.

The Believer's Cross

Then Jesus told his disciples, "If anyone would come after me, let him deny himself and take up his cross and follow me. For whoever would save his life will lose it, but whoever loses his life for my sake will find it. For what will it profit a man if he gains the whole world and forfeits his soul? Or what shall a man give in return for his soul?" (Matthew 16:24–26)

Text

Matthew 16:24–26

Truth

Each follower of Jesus embraces his own cross out of gratitude to Christ.

Hymn: "When I Survey the Wondrous Cross"

When I survey the wondrous cross
On which the Prince of glory died,

My richest gain I count but loss,
And pour contempt on all my pride.

Forbid it, Lord, that I should boast,
Save in the death of Christ my God:
All the vain things that charm me most,
I sacrifice them to his blood.

See, from his head, his hands, his feet,
Sorrow and love flow mingled down:
Did e'er such love and sorrow meet,
Or thorns compose so rich a crown?

Were the whole realm of nature mine,
That were a present far too small;
Love so amazing, so divine,
Demands my soul, my life, my all.

—Isaac Watts, 1707

Opening Prayer

Our Father and God, as we survey the wondrous cross, we are taken aback by its splendor, the paradox of love and sorrow flowing mingled down from the body of our Lord Jesus Christ. The vain things of the world charm us, and our commitment to you is less than our all. Teach us from your Word by your Spirit how to embrace our cross, not just today, but for the remainder of our lives. With gratitude. Amen.

Questions for Study and Discussion

▶ READ MATTHEW 16:24–26

1. In your own words, explain Jesus' requirements for coming after him.

▶ READ ROMANS 12:1–2; 1 CORINTHIANS 6:19–20; AND PHILIPPIANS 2:5–7

2. How does Jesus' example and work help you to understand what your cross entails?

3. Give examples of what it means that you were bought by Christ and now belong to him.

4. How is being a living sacrifice related to following Jesus and taking up your cross?

► READ GALATIANS 2:20; AND EPHESIANS 1:19–20

5. How is Jesus' resurrection significant to your new life in Christ?

6. Give an example of how you no longer live but Christ lives in you.

▶ READ 2 CORINTHIANS 5:17–21

7. What is the message of reconciliation? Who needs to be reconciled?

8. What can you do to be a minister of reconciliation? Give specific examples.

▶ READ JOHN 17:14 AND HEBREWS 12:1–3

9. What hardship might you experience if you deny yourself, take up your cross, and follow Jesus? How does your hardship compare to Jesus' suffering for you?

10. Give specific examples of how you might bring glory to God in your hardships.

11. How does Paul explain your hardships in 2 Corinthians 4:17? Do you agree?

12. From the following verses, what joy can you anticipate if you deny yourself, take up your cross, and follow Jesus?

    a. Matthew 11:28–30; Hebrews 2:18

    b. Matthew 25:23

c. John 17:22, 24; 1 John 3:2

d. 1 Thessalonians 2:13–14

e. Romans 8:28–30; Philippians 1:6; Revelation 21:27

f. 1 Corinthians 15:36–57; Revelation 21:4

13. Do all Christians have the same cross to carry? Explain your answer, using any verses from Scripture.

14. Which words of "When I Survey the Wondrous Cross" help you to understand what it means to deny yourself, take up your cross, and follow Jesus? Write a prayer of commitment based on them.

Commentary

Remembering everything you have learned before a test is challenging. I remember classmates staying up all night drinking coffee in order to cram for a final exam. Sadly, many of them slept through the test. Passing life's "pop tests" requires study, not cramming.

When we eat, we take a small bite, chew it, and swallow it to ingest what we have chewed; then it works through our digestive system, giving us strength for the day. The food we ingest and digest is what gives us strength. The same is true for the Word of God. That is why this study offers questions that require you to think deeply, instead of multiple choices that you can guess easily. You are chewing on the Word of God; as you swallow it for your own life, you are ingesting it into your person and subconsciously digesting it. This progressively becomes the way you approach your life. Keep chewing even when it is tough. God will strengthen you for the days ahead.

The cross of Jesus Christ is the central event of God's overarching historical plan to redeem a people for himself. He did so by providing the perfect sacrifice for the forgiveness of sin and the scapegoat who would take away their guilt—his Son, the Lord Jesus Christ. Without the cross of Christ, there is no resurrection, no redemption for sinners, no eternal life, no hope, and no heaven. Where do you and I fit into God's plan? Through faith in Christ and out of gratitude for all he has done for us, we follow Jesus. But what does that look like?

Jesus' Mandate

Jesus said, "If anyone would come after me, let him deny himself and take up his cross and follow me" (Matthew 16:24). Let us consider his statement phrase by phrase, applying it to you.

231

Deny Yourself

You claim no right to yourself or to anything you have or desire, including your favorite indulgence (sin). You renounce your right to yourself, self-effort, and moral goodness. You come to the end of yourself; this is the biggest hurdle for most. You deny that you can make it to God on your own efforts. You acknowledge that you cannot save yourself no matter how hard you try. You purpose to be absolutely his. Will you live for the glory of God, or are you more concerned about yourself? Will you live for his kingdom or for your comfort and things?

Take Up Your Cross

The cross is an instrument of death, prescribed by the highest government; it declares that you are guilty before a higher tribunal than yourself. Your life is on the death march as you acknowledge that you are guilty before the holy Creator. You willingly carry the cross that God ordains for you, whatever he providentially puts in your life. Your cross is God's instrument for sanctifying and equipping you for the ministry of reconciliation entrusted to all believers.

Follow Jesus

You follow Jesus at all times, even when you know not where, when, or how. You do whatever he says even when you do not understand why. Jesus responded to mocking, hostility, and persecution by doing what he had taught his disciples: "love your enemies and pray for those who persecute you" (Matthew 5:44). He prayed for their forgiveness. Paul explained this kingdom truth, "Be kind to one another, tenderhearted, forgiving one another, as God in Christ forgave you" (Ephesians 4:32).

The greatest in Jesus' kingdom is the one who humbly takes the lowest place and serves others (Mark 9:35). Jesus demonstrated this teaching by washing his disciples' feet, a task of the lowest servant (John 13:3–16).

Make no mistake. To follow Jesus will cost you your life. He said, "For whoever would save his life will lose it, but whoever loses his life for my sake will find it" (Matthew 16:25). Embrace this great exchange by faith: your sin is laid on Christ while his perfect life and righteousness are credited to you. This is not a reward for your righteousness but God's gracious gift for the guilty whose best efforts are like a polluted garment (Isaiah 64:6). Real life is living by Christ's power, not by your feeble attempts to do what is right before God.

Believers' Response

Comparison with Jesus' Cross

Jesus' cross was God's purpose for Jesus to redeem sinful people by reconciling them to God. Jesus' cross meant death for him in order to give eternal life to others. You might think of your cross as what God asks you to do to bring Christ, who is eternal life, to others. This means that your cross is God's purpose for you in his overarching plan of redeeming a people for himself. It includes being made progressively more like Jesus in preparation for heaven. It also means participating in Jesus' giving life to others through you. What an incredible purpose for life! Let us draw some parallels from Jesus' cross.

Jesus left his glory in heaven to come to earth as a true man. He left heaven to take on a human body restricted by time and space in order to become one of us (Philippians 2:5–7). There is no other perfect human, for all have sinned and fallen short of God's glory (Romans 3:23).

Your cross means leaving behind your perceived right to yourself and denying yourself. You look not only to your own interests but also to the interests of others (Philippians 2:4). You give up your right to set the course of your life. You embrace that God, not you, writes the script for your life. Your biography will contain some chapters you would not have chosen to include. For you have been bought by Christ at the cost of his precious blood (1 Corinthians 6:20). You are no longer your own. You belong to Jesus and willingly follow his example of submitting yourself to God.

Jesus' cross cost him his human life. Jesus Christ actually died on the cross. He could not have saved you if he had not died.

Your cross means death. When Christ died, you died with him.

> For the love of Christ controls us, because we have concluded this: that one has died for all, therefore all have died; and he died for all, that those who live might no longer live for themselves but for him who for their sake died and was raised. (2 Corinthians 5:14–15)

You are dead to the world, to sin, and to your own hopes, dreams, weaknesses, strengths, and perceived needs for people, things, recognition, and so on. Your cross may or may not mean physical death for Christ's kingdom. However, the death of your former way of life must happen before God can replace it with his plans for you, which are better than you could ever imagine.

Jesus' cross brought life to others. It made possible his resurrection, ascension, and coronation. Jesus Christ could not have saved us if he had remained dead.

Your cross brings life to others. The same power that raised Jesus from the dead is what raised you from being dead in sin to being alive in Christ (Ephesians 1:19–20). He has given you a new life and the power of his Spirit to live for him. He has entrusted you with the message of reconciliation to God. You are an ambassador for Christ to a lost and dying world, telling others how he took God's judgment of your trespasses and sins in your place (2 Corinthians 5:17–21). An ambassador lives in a foreign land and represents his king, leader, and country. If you are in Christ, your home is heaven; you are an alien living in the foreign land of this earth and representing Christ to those around you. This is part of each believer's cross. By God's grace alone, you have a part in his raising others to eternal life through faith alone in Christ alone.

Jesus was the only atoning sacrifice for sin. No one else could satisfy God's just wrath against sin. You cannot atone for your sin or for another's sin. However, in view of God's mercies to you in Christ, you are called to be a living sacrifice (Romans 1:1–12:1). How? In Christ, you follow his desires that are within you through his Holy Spirit. As you delight in him, he will give you his desires (Psalm 37:4). In Christ, your mind resists tempting thoughts that move temptation into sin; your eyes reject sights that are impure or evil; your mouth speaks words from your new heart; your hands and feet go places that please God.

Have you ever offered your body (mind, eyes, ears, lips, hands, feet, and so on) as a living sacrifice to God? Will you write today's date next to Romans 12:1–2 in your Bible? If so, then write, "Dear God, here I am. I am yours no matter the cost. I want to be transformed by renewing my mind." God will direct your path as you embark on your commitment to be a living sacrifice, a privilege that leads to joy.

Jesus' cross required endurance with joy. What if Jesus had stopped in the middle of the cross because it was too hard? We would have no hope! He endured the cross for the joy set before him (Hebrews 12:1–2). His joy was the satisfaction of completing the work that the Father gave him on earth: conquering sin and death, redeeming those whom God gave him, giving them eternal life, and returning to heaven with them as his prize (Isaiah 53:10–12; John 17:24). His cross was agonizing, it meant great pain, it meant death, it meant bearing God's wrath, but it was worth it.

Your cross will require endurance. Your sanctification, the process by which you now live, is by faith in God's Word, which exhorts us to press on, strive, work, and continue (Philippians 3:12–14). However, Jesus is your helper and advocate (1 John 2:1) and his Spirit is within you. Jesus knows all that you encounter because he has gone before you (Hebrews 2:18). He will help you to carry your cross all the way to the end. Whatever it takes will be worth the joy that awaits you. Looking to Jesus will keep you from growing weary or fainthearted (Hebrews 12:3).

Many people give their lives to causes that may be gratifying for the short term but are worthless in God's economy. In fact, they may be working against God. What cause consumes your thoughts, emotions, time, energy, finances, and prayers? How much is it worth in God's kingdom purposes?

Anticipated Joy

What joy can you anticipate? Several promises belong to Christ's redeemed:

Jesus' presence. You will be with Jesus where he is, seeing his glory and being like him (John 17:22, 24; 1 John 3:2). Today, you have his presence in you through the Holy Spirit.

Jesus' commendation. Those who have faithfully invested Jesus' resources for his kingdom will hear, "Well done, good and faithful servant" (Matthew 25:23). They will enter into his joy.

Fruitfulness. Some people will receive the Word of God, which they hear from you. They will accept it not as your word but as what it really is, the Word of God, which is at work in them. You will rejoice with them in heaven (1 Thessalonians 2:13–14).

Glorification, the absence of sin and suffering. "Those whom he predestined he also called, and those whom he called he also justified, and those whom he justified he also glorified" (Romans 8:30). "He who began a good work in you will bring it to completion at the day of Jesus Christ" (Philippians 1:6). You will no longer be plagued by temptation, sin, and death in the new heaven and new earth (Revelation 21:27). God promises his children that any affliction they endure on earth will be eclipsed by the glory they may expect in heaven. "For this light momentary affliction is preparing for us an eternal weight of glory beyond all comparison" (2 Corinthians 4:17). "He will wipe away every tear from their eyes, and death shall be no more, neither shall there be mourning, nor crying, nor pain anymore, for the former things have passed away" (Revelation 21:4).

A resurrected, imperishable body. This new body will be eternal, imperishable, and glorified like Jesus' resurrected body (1 Corinthians 15:36–57). The bodily resurrection of Jesus is crucial. Because he was raised in a body (not just spiritually), we also will be raised in a body.

Kingdom Privileges

Speaking the Truth

God's call. In every age, God uses Jesus' disciples to call people to himself. Each of us shares this task in taking up our cross. How do we call others to God? We are being prepared to do so through this Bible study—chewing on God's Word, especially the tough parts, ingesting it into our lives, and being transformed by it. God's powerful Word does God's work in this world. God's Spirit takes God's Word and creates God's people. Therefore, we spread God's Word with our mouths, through our lives, and through support of our churches and other ministries. God does the work of regeneration and transformation; our task is to spread the truth in word and deed about who Jesus is and what he has done. Ask God daily where, what, and with whom you are to speak for Jesus. Speak this week to your pastor about how you can be involved in the work entrusted to your church.

Message of reconciliation. All of us are called to be messengers of reconciliation. We have the same message, yet there is diversity in our crosses. God has crafted your cross exactly for you. It will involve people, gifts, talents, and circumstances unique to you. With whom might you share this message?

> Mat is aboard a Boeing 777, racing to Los Angeles across the Pacific Ocean. "God's call to teach his magnificent Word has taken me to places globally—from southern skies to northern lights, from heat waves to snow. Why am I willing to go wherever, whenever, to whoever? A settled trust in God, who drew me to himself, saved me through no effort of my own, and called me to serve him in ways beyond my imagination. In a peculiar reversal, as I pour myself into others, God pours himself into me. God is bringing me to BSF (Bible Study Fellowship) global headquarters for training to teach and lead a BSF class in Melbourne, Australia. This heavy responsibility will require focus, time, and effort. Some other ministry opportunities will be curtailed. God will stretch me, but I get front row seats to see God work and glorify himself as others hear the message of reconciliation. He who fills my cup to overflowing will steady my hand to pour his blessings into others."

Serving Others

Caring for family members. Perhaps you have grown children who pay their own bills and own their own homes. You might have thought, "Now I have time for myself." However, your aging parents take up all "your" time. Your time actually belongs to God; he bought it for himself and his purposes. Caring for an ill or aging parent can be emotionally draining, but it is spreading God's love to the one who gave you birth. I watched my husband and his sister, Totsie, devote themselves wholeheartedly for ten years to care for their aging parents. Totsie retired early to be available whenever needed—giving time, showing lovingkindness, and being an advocate for their health care, to name but a few things. They lived "honor your father and your mother" to the fullest extent.

Showing hospitality. A simple meal in your home provides opportunity for conversation about Jesus, the only food that satisfies.

Passing the faith. Teaching children in your church is an investment in the kingdom of God with eternal benefits for you, the children, their families, and your church. Who knows how God might use one of those children to further his kingdom?

Assisting in ministry. Helping another in his or her ministry may include dying to your own ideas about leading but finding joy in embracing the role of assistant.

Loving others. Showing love in practical ways demonstrates how Christ has loved you and given his life for you. Loving an unlovely person communicates that God's love is unconditional. It opens the way for you to explain God's love demonstrated in Christ's atoning sacrifice.

What have you been doing or will you begin to do today to serve others?

Knowing God's Will

God's individual. Knowing God's will begins with you. God will show you his will as you offer yourself to him. You will find that God's will is good and pleasing to your soul.

God's family. God has a plan of redemption, and each of us has a place in it. Peter described God's redeemed as a building of "living stones . . . being built up as a spiritual house, to be a holy priesthood, to offer spiritual sacrifices acceptable to God through Jesus Christ" (1 Peter 2:5). In a stone building, each individual stone has a place. However, it requires a rock hammer or chisel in the hand of the master rock mason to make each one fit into the whole. Ouch! Sometimes it hurts, but the crafted and completed building brings glory and honor to the craftsman. God, the builder, wants you. He is fitting you for the whole. Will you thank him for whatever he sends your way to make you fit into his family—his redeemed, who look like his Son, the Lord Jesus Christ?

God's ownership. God has the right to your life because he created you and redeemed you for himself. He has the authority to tell you to live a life of sacrifice—self-denial, taking up a cross, following Jesus—for him and his glory. Love so amazing, so divine, demands your soul, your life, and your all.

God's reward. You will need endurance to offer yourself as a living sacrifice to God. But, like Christ, for the joy set before you, you will carry your cross all the way to glory. You will be satisfied as you hear his commendation. You will see him as he is because you will be like him. You will see others who are the fruit of your labor. You will rejoice that you will never again experience the sorrow of the presence of sin. The light and momentary afflictions of this life will be erased by the glory that will be yours eternally in Christ.

Does God have you? If God has you, you have everything. You have a purpose: to glorify God and proclaim the crucified and risen Christ who was sent to be the atoning sacrifice for your sins and to give you new life. When you stand before him in glory, you will see what you know now by faith: you belong to him and not to yourself. Casting your crowns, which are his, at his feet, will be your reward.

Embracing Your Cross

God has a cross for you that will require denying yourself and will mean death to your ways and dreams in order to live for Christ. It is useless to try to exchange your cross for another or to envy someone else's cross. God has determined for you what will best glorify him and will accomplish his purpose for your holiness. Grumbling against God or running from his will is futile, ending in empty pursuits that rob you of joy. Will you embrace your cross out of gratitude to Christ for his cross? You cannot claim to follow Jesus, to be a Christian, if you do not. If you do, you will find blessing upon blessing, grace upon grace, and incomparable joy.

The Changed Cross

It was a time of sadness—and my heart,
Although it knew and loved the better part,
Felt wearied with the conflict and the strife,
And all the needful discipline of life.

And while I thought on these—as given to me,
My trial-tests of faith and love to be,
It seemed as if I never could be sure
That faithful to the end I should endure.

And thus, no longer trusting to His might
Who says, "We walk by faith and not by sight,"
Doubting—and almost yielding to despair,
The thought arose, *My cross I cannot bear!*

Far heavier its weight must surely be
Than those of others which I daily see;
Oh, if I might another burden choose,
Methinks I should not fear my crown to lose.

A solemn silence reigned on all around,
E'en nature's voices uttered not a sound;
The evening shadows seemed of peace to tell,
And sleep upon my weary spirit fell.

A moment's pause—and then a heavenly light
Beamed full upon my wondering, raptured sight;
Angels on silvery wings seemed everywhere,
And angels' music thrilled the balmy air.

Then One more fair than all the rest to see,
One to whom all the others bowed the knee,
Came gently to me as I trembling lay,
And, "Follow me," He said, "I am the Way."

Then speaking thus, He led me far above,
And there, beneath a canopy of love,
Crosses of diverse shape and size were seen,
Larger and smaller than mine own had been.

And one there was most beauteous to behold—
A little one, with jewels set in gold;
Ah, this, methought, I can with comfort wear,
For it will be an easy one to bear.

And so the little cross I quickly took;
But all at once my frame beneath it shook—
The sparkling jewels, fair were they to *see*,
But far too heavy was their *weight* for me.

This may not be, I cried, and looked again
To see if any there could ease my pain;
But one by one I passed them slowly by,
Till on a lovely one I cast my eye.

Fair flowers around its sculptured form entwined,
And grace and beauty seemed in it combined;
Wondering I gazed—and still I wondered more
To think so many should have passed it o'er.

But oh, that form so beautiful to see,
Soon made its hidden sorrows known to me;—
Thorns lay beneath those flowers and colours fair;
Sorrowing I said, This cross I may not bear.

And so it was with each and all around,
Not one to suit my *need* could there be found;
Weeping, I laid each heavy burden down,
As my Guide gently said, "No cross—no crown."

At length to Him I raised my saddened heart;
He knew its sorrows, bid its doubts depart,—
"Be not afraid," He said, "but trust in me,
My perfect love shall now be shown to thee."

And then, with lightened eyes and willing feet,
Again I turned my earthly cross to meet,
With forward footsteps, turning not aside,
For fear some hidden evil might betide.

And there, in the prepared, appointed way,
Listening to hear, and ready to obey,
A cross I quickly found of plainest form,
With only words of love inscribed thereon.

With thankfulness I raised it from the rest,
And joyfully acknowledged it the best;
The *only* one of all the many there,
That I could feel was *good* for me to bear;

And while I thus my chosen one confessed,
I saw a heavenly brightness on it rest,
And as I bent my burden to sustain,
I recognized my own old cross again!

But oh, how different did it seem to be,
Now I had learned its preciousness to see!
No longer could I unbelieving say,
Perhaps another is a better way.

Ah, no! henceforth my one desire shall be
That He who knows me best should choose for me;
And so, whate'er His love sees good to send,
I'll trust is best—because He knows the end.

> "For my thoughts are not your thoughts,
> neither are your ways my ways, saith the
> Lord."—*Isa.* lv. 8. [Isaiah 55:8 KJV]

> For I know the thoughts that I think
> toward you, saith the Lord, thoughts
> of peace, and not of evil, to give you an
> EXPECTED END."—*Jer.* xxix. 11. [Jeremiah 29:11 KJV]

And when that happy time shall come,
    Of endless peace and rest,
We shall look back upon our path,
    And say, *It was the best.*[1]

---

1. Mrs. Charles Hobart, *The Changed Cross*, 20th ed. (London: Wells Gardner, Darton, & Co., n.d.)

Closing Prayer

Sovereign, all-wise God, thank you that your way is always best. Please renew my mind, change my priorities, and cause me to hate what you hate and love what you love. Help me to understand that in you, I am called to live by the extraordinary power of your Spirit. May I boast only in you, Lord Jesus, and in the work you have done for me, not in my own accomplishments. If the sun, moon, stars, galaxies, earth, animals, plants, gold, silver, jewels, and all natural resources were mine, that would be a present far too small for you. Help me to embrace my cross by being your messenger of reconciliation to a lost and dying world and by living in the circumstances in which you place me for the glory of your name and the furtherance of your kingdom. May I be a diligent student of you, Lord Jesus, that I may by your grace and the power of your Spirit follow your example. I give you my soul, my life, my all for the joy set before me. Amen.

Transformed by the Cross

I appeal to you therefore, brothers, by the mercies of God, to present your bodies as a living sacrifice, holy and acceptable to God, which is your spiritual worship. Do not be conformed to this world, but be transformed by the renewal of your mind, that by testing you may discern what is the will of God, what is good and acceptable and perfect. (Romans 12:1–2)

Texts

Romans 12:1–2
Hebrews 12:1–2

Truth

Being a living sacrifice is a life-transforming process.

Hymn: "Amazing Grace"

Amazing grace!—how sweet the sound—
That saved a wretch like me!
I once was lost, but now am found,
Was blind, but now I see.

'Twas grace that taught my heart to fear,
And grace my fears relieved;
How precious did that grace appear
The hour I first believed!

Thro' many dangers, toils, and snares,
I have already come;
'Tis grace has brought me safe thus far,
And grace will lead me home.

The Lord has promised good to me,
His Word my hope secures;
He will my shield and portion be,
As long as life endures.

And when this flesh and heart shall fail,
And mortal life shall cease,
I shall possess within the veil
A life of joy and peace.

When we've been there ten thousand years,
Bright shining as the sun,
We've no less days to sing God's praise
Than when we've first begun.

—Stanzas 1–5: John Newton, 1779
Stanza 6: A Collection of Sacred Ballads, 1790

Opening Prayer

Gracious God, your amazing grace has taught our hearts to fear but has then relieved those fears. We are in awe of all that our salvation involved, our need for it, your gracious provision of it, and your love that motivated it. May we never lose sight of the beautiful meaning of the cross as we face dangers, toils, and snares in this life. Keep our minds focused on your Word, which secures our hope. Stir our hearts to anticipate eternally praising you. Empower us to hold out this message of hope to a lost and dying world. In Jesus' mighty and precious name. Amen.

Questions for Study and Discussion

▶ **REVIEW PAST LESSONS**

1. For each of the following lessons, state simply in your own words one fact or truth about the cross that you have found helpful and have applied to your life. How is your life different because you applied the truth?

a. The Promise of the Cross

b. The Person on the Cross

c. The Prayers Leading to the Cross

d. The Pain of the Cross

e. The Perfection of the Cross

f. The People at the Cross

g. The Words from the Cross

h. The Power of the Cross

i. The Believer's Cross

2. What truths have changed your thinking about God, Jesus, and yourself? How have they changed your attitude or priorities?

3. How has your assurance of God's love for you grown through the study?

4. Give specific examples of how God's love has motivated you to express love to him.

▶ CONTEMPLATE THE WORDS OF THE SCRIPTURES MENTIONED BELOW ALONG WITH THE VERSES OF THE HYMN "WHEN I SURVEY THE WONDROUS CROSS" (LESSON 10) TO ANSWER THE FOLLOWING QUESTIONS

5. Read verse 1 of the hymn with Philippians 3:7–11. What have you counted as loss compared to gaining Christ?

6. Read verse 2 of the hymn and Philippians 3:12–16. What specific, vain things that charm you most are you willing to sacrifice because Jesus died for you?

7. Read verse 3 of the hymn and Galatians 2:19–20. How would you explain the mingling of sorrow and love in Jesus' cross for you?

8. Read verse 4 of the hymn and Romans 12:1–2. Describe the spiritual worship that is appropriate following your survey of Jesus' cross.

▶ **DIG DEEPLY**

9. For one day, write down the subjects that fill your thoughts. What did you find surprising? How might the preoccupation of your thoughts rob you of the joy of Jesus?

10. How do these life changes make you want to tell others about the cross? How might you be able to do so?

Commentary

Did you think at the beginning of this study, "How am I going to spend so much time on this one subject?" Are you still there? Or have you concluded that there is more to this than you ever realized? Why spend so much time talking about the cross of Jesus Christ? Is this masochistic or sadistic? Do we just enjoy punishing ourselves with our guilt and sorrow? Perspective is necessary to understand true life and the life of a Christian. The cross of Christ provides that necessary perspective.

Jesus' suffering was intense from the time of his incarnation until his final words from the cross. He left the throne room of heaven to be born a human in a stable—not even room for him in an inn! He endured rejection and threats to his life. He faced temptation in every way yet without sin. He, the Lord of creation, had to carry his own cross after having been brutally tortured, mocked, and unjustly condemned. He was taken outside the city to be crucified between two criminals in the place where trash was dumped. He was made to suffer before those who loved him.

We do not study the cross to leave us in despair or to drive us to depression. Rather, we study it to open our eyes to our great need for Christ, the cost of our redemption to God, and his love for us. We are sinful human beings who have no right to enter into his holy presence. He has made the only acceptable way to approach him; that way is the cross of Christ.

Important Truths

We have focused on the defining moment in history that gives meaning for today and hope for tomorrow: the cross of Jesus Christ. We have learned several important truths.

- Jesus' suffering was necessary and sufficient to save us from our sin and to satisfy God's wrath.
- Sin is so bad that it required Christ's suffering and death. God did not give him anything more than was required; neither did he give him anything less.
- Jesus' suffering demonstrated the enormousness of God's love for us and our value to him. The cross is the eraser for our thoughts of worthlessness and self-exaltation.
- Jesus endured the cross while anticipating his joyful return to his Father in glory accompanied by his redeemed, glorified people. We have the assurance that Jesus prayed for our glorification! What great hope this brings in the midst of our crazy world.

Christians have hope for present satisfaction and eternal joy. We will see Jesus and be with him where he is. Our ears will hear him commend us for our faithful service. We will meet those who believed in him as a result of our testimony. No longer will we be plagued with sin, for sin will no longer be present in our glorified, resurrected, and imperishable bodies. We will be reunited with loved ones who died in Christ.

Reasons for Not Having Joy

Why, then, do we not always feel joyful? What robs us of joy?

Not Controlled by the Holy Spirit

Joy is a fruit of the Holy Spirit (Galatians 5:16–26). An absence of joy means that our desires and thoughts are not controlled by him. What is filling your mind and therefore ruling your heart?

Worry. We worry about rejection, the future, the unknown, pain, failure, and death. The bottom line of worry is unbelief; we do not believe that God will be there for us. What if God does not rescue me or help me as I think he should? To confess worry as unbelief is to be lifted out of it into trust.

Envy. We envy others for their position, power, possessions, physical attractiveness, ability, and so on. The root of envy is covetousness, which is idolatry (Colossians 3:5). Whatever we covet is an idol, something we think we need more than God to make us happy.

Pride. Pride is thinking that we know better than God. What does pride look like? Insisting on our own way over God's and

260

others', a critical spirit, nitpicking, bragging, and so on. Pride heads the list of things that God hates (Proverbs 6:16–19). Pride exalts us and our ideas above God and his sovereign will. We follow Adam and Eve's sin in thinking we can determine what is good and what is evil apart from God (Genesis 3).

Discontent. Discontent is seen in ingratitude, dissatisfaction, and unrealistic and unmet expectations. Advertisements aim to create discontent and to stir up desires for what we think we need and do not have. Discontent doubts God's goodness and love, thinking that he does not give us what we need. Because God loves us, he does not give us everything we think we need. If we got what we deserve, we would get God's wrath! Instead, God gives us what we do not deserve— his mercy. We must remind ourselves that God has given us everything we need in Christ. All his provisions are reasons to thank him.

Worldliness. Our world values hedonism, narcissism, materialism, consumerism, and entitlement. Love for the world system apart from God is not from him; it is the antithesis of God's purpose for his people (1 John 2:15–17). Why love what is passing away when you can turn your affections to what is eternal?

Not Conditioned for Life's Race

We also are not joyful because we are not conditioned for life's race. Following Christ continues for the remainder of our earthly lives. The path is often uphill or against the current of the world. Several truths are worth committing to memory for recall when strength seems small:

The Christian journey is a lifelong marathon. Running a marathon requires a training program and commitment to cross the finish line. Both the training and the race require endurance, perseverance, and discipline. Most runners struggle at some point with wondering if they can make it to the finish line. Setting small goals helps them. Thinking about how far they have left is not wise. The same is true for Christians in their race to the finish line. The marathon prize is awarded at the end of life, not after a few weeks of trying to see whether we like it. We need perseverance to press on and discipline to do what is right at the right time and in the right way. Mental focus is key to winning the spiritual war. The New Testament tells us to strive, press on, make every effort, and so on. We need God's power to do this. However, God promises to take us to the finish line (Philippians 1:6). We persevere through faith in Jesus Christ, who has gone before us.

Sanctification is God's daily transformation of the life of a believer, ending in glorification in heaven. Sanctification is God's application of the gospel to our lives. God uses people, circumstances, surprises, and disappointments in life to make us more like Jesus. Is that your goal? For what do you pray? Comfort? Healing? Wealth? Or sanctification no matter the cost?

Only Jesus can satisfy your soul. Jesus alone can meet your needs and satisfy your longings. If you look to anyone or anything else, you will lose heart, grow weary, and faint. Do you feel like that? Take a look at who and what is filling your time and ruling your heart. Where does Jesus fit? You cannot squeeze him into your life after everything else. He must be first, even before your service for him.

God's children are to live by faith. Living by faith means more than believing *in* God. Faith means believing God. His Word and ways are trustworthy.

God's purpose for his children is that we become like his Son (Romans 8:28–30). God is more concerned for our holiness than for our present comfort, worldly acclaim, power, health, wealth, and so on. He knows what is best for us to accomplish his purpose. It is foolish and a waste of time and energy to seek another way.

Success in God's kingdom is based on faithfulness. God measures success differently from the world. He commends faithfulness (Matthew 25:21). Some faithful missionaries have given their lives without seeing a single convert to Christ. Only after they are gone do others reap what they have sown. Were they successful? Yes, by God's standards.

Reasons for Joy

God's Unchanging Truth

The cross is based on God's promises. They were foretold in the Old Testament and reiterated and explained in the New Testament. Jesus kept these promises in his mind throughout his life of suffering and as he approached the cross. God's promises and his fulfillment of God's plan gave him joy. They also give us joy. Knowing Bible truth through memorization of verses and study of God's character and ways gives us treasures stored in our minds and hearts to meet future needs.

Christ's Perfect Person and Work

Jesus of Nazareth, the person who died on the cross, was no ordinary man. He was both fully God and fully man, the only person worthy of being the sacrifice for our sins. He claimed to be God and his works verified his claims.

Jesus demonstrated how to pray. His prayers demonstrated the joy that he had as he anticipated his return to his throne in heaven, taking with him the people he redeemed. Our glorification was part of the joy he sought in prayer during the last night of his life, before he faced the agonizing prayer in Gethsemane. His example teaches us how to pray. We begin with God's promises regarding the future to find strength for the perils of the moment and power to submit to God's will in them.

The people staying close to Jesus received the greatest blessing. They heard Jesus' words of comfort and his call to help others.

God's call for Carl and Bonnie changed when they adopted their one-year-old, severely handicapped grandson. Bonnie writes, "We were presented with an incredible, life-changing future. I knew this was out of my realm of mothering and definitely out of my comfort zone, but it was the right decision. For seven years, I have discovered that it is not Nicholas who needs me; it is I who needs Nicholas. Life is hard physically, mentally, and emotionally, but the precious rewards and joys are immeasurable by anyone's standards. Caring for one who is totally dependent on me for everything in his life has shown me how I am to live totally dependent on God. When this precious child of God looks up at me with total adoration and love, my heart melts. That keeps me going when life gets tough."

The words of Jesus from the cross showed his heart's desire and life mission. He reached out to people in need with salvation and help, even in his agonizing pain. He demonstrated for us what life in his kingdom looks like.

Jesus' pain was unmatched by any pain that humans experience. Many people died of crucifixion and were scourged, beaten, and mocked. He alone endured hell in our place, as the fullness of God's wrath was poured out on him as he hung on the cross. His cry, "My God, my God, why have you forsaken me?" was met with silence as he experienced the wrath of God for the sins of those who receive him as their Savior.

The people who reject Jesus will experience God's wrath. Those who die apart from Christ will receive what they deserve—eternal anguish. If they cry out to God, there will be no words of comfort. They will be met with silence and the continuous outpouring of God's wrath. No one can look at Jesus on the cross and remain neutral. To postpone commitment to Jesus is to reject him and choose hell.

The cross was necessary for Jesus to die and be buried, so he could be raised for our justification. My sins were imputed to him, and his perfect righteous life was imputed to me. This is my hope: to live in a new way that anticipates the hope of heaven and the power over sin in my present life. I have power to live in a way I could not before I received him and his atonement for me. Do you have that assurance?

The cross was perfect in every way. It is what God planned as the only way we could approach him and live in his presence.

Biblical Response to the Cross

Matthew 16:24–26

Then Jesus told his disciples, "If anyone would come after me, let him deny himself and take up his cross and follow me. For whoever would save his life will lose it, but whoever loses his life for my sake will find it. For what will it profit a man if he gains the whole world and forfeits his soul? Or what shall a man give in return for his soul?"

As I retired from my involvement with BSF, some people said to me, "I guess you're just going to sleep in, hang out, and enjoy yourself." I replied, "I doubt I will sleep in, but I do intend to enjoy what I have done for the past forty years. God has entrusted much to me and has given me a love for him, his Word, and the study of it. The cross I have gladly taken is to know God, study carefully, and help others to know him as well."

Romans 12:1–2

I appeal to you therefore, brothers, by the mercies of God, to present your bodies as a living sacrifice, holy and acceptable to God, which is your spiritual worship. Do not be conformed to this world, but be transformed by the renewal of your mind, that by testing you may discern what is the will of God, what is good and acceptable and perfect.

Our mind, eyes, ears, heart, hands, and feet are to be presented to God while we are alive. This requires mind renewal. Our default mode is following our flesh, the world, and empty pursuits. When God regenerated us, we entered the process of changing our ways of thinking by renewing our mind with his Word. Why? That we may have the freedom to know and do whatever God entrusts to us, and to discover that it is good, acceptable, and perfect.

Philippians 3:7, 10–14

But whatever gain I had, I counted as loss for the sake of Christ . . . that I may know him and the power of his resurrection, and may share his sufferings, becoming like him in his death, that by any means possible I may attain the resurrection from the dead.

Not that I have already obtained this or am already perfect, but I press on to make it my own, because Christ Jesus has made me his own . . . forgetting what lies behind and straining forward to what lies ahead, I press on toward the goal for the prize of the upward call of God in Christ Jesus.

Salvation from the penalty and guilt of sin is only the beginning. The life of a Christian is a battlefield against our enemies: the Devil, the world, and our flesh. We press on through the power of the Holy Spirit to be saved from the power of sin (Romans 8). The goal is to be ready for our eternal sin-free home, saved from the very presence of sin. Life is not always neat and tidy in this battle against sin. This is the upward call of God in Christ Jesus for us, and God is working to bring it about one step at a time.

Barb decided to run a marathon. Little did she know it would be training for living through an intense family conflict that required perseverance and trust in God's sovereign and good will for her and her family's sanctification. "Suddenly, we ordinary people were watching our gifted daughter caught up in a nightmare with CPS, court, jail, and broken judicial systems. Yet God was sovereign over all of it. It was painful and humiliating to watch her be arrested and to think of her spending the night within the confines of a cold concrete holding cell in the county jail. Her husband falsely accused her of physical assault—a felony charge that, if she were found guilty, carried a minimum five-year prison sentence. The horror of her two young children being taken from her involved our entire family. For nine months, her father and I had custody of them. She could see them but not take them home. Our new normal included juggling children, meals, and jobs and sharing the load with our son, daughter-in-law, and their five boys. Blessedly, the court absolved her of all guilt and awarded her full custody; the children are at home with her. We are trying to determine our new normal.

"Is our story over? No, we have finished one chapter but realize that this is part of God's teaching us about him. We have learned some important truths. God demonstrates his presence and goodness in the midst of the pain. In his hands, what we think is horrible is what he uses to produce what we most need. He knows the degree of sandpaper to use on each of us. We talk about peace and submission to God being good when everything is working out to our comfort and satisfaction. We agree that we need a fair amount of trouble, but we think we should be instantly holy. What happens when we face God's coarse sandpaper on us and our children? We are learning that it is good because it is bearing eternal fruit.

"The longer I walk with Jesus, the more I see that nothing can be changed without risking the promised end. This is the connection to my marathon training. The race does not end quickly. Perseverance is required to cross the line. On my first race I heard, 'You have one-and-a-half miles to go!' I thought, 'If Jesus is the prize, I would crawl on my belly and elbows to get there.' Jesus is the prize, and we are his prize that he won on the cross. He is our present help in times of our light and momentary afflictions, which are nothing compared to the glory that will be ours when we see him face to face."

Hebrews 10:19, 21–24

Therefore, brothers, since we have confidence to enter the holy places by the blood of Jesus . . . and since we have a great priest over the house of God, let us draw near with a true heart in full assurance of faith. . . . Let us hold fast the confession of our hope without wavering, for he who promised is faithful. And let us consider how to stir up one another to love and good works.

Living for Jesus includes confidence to approach God with reverence, gratitude, a clean conscience, and prayers offered in faith. We meet with other Christians to encourage one another to love God and people. We stir up one another to serve God in anticipation of Jesus' return in glory. Where are you doing this?

2 Corinthians 5:17–18, 20

Therefore, if anyone is in Christ, he is a new creation. The old has passed away; behold, the new has come. All this is from God, who through Christ reconciled us to himself and gave us the ministry of reconciliation. . . . Therefore, we are ambassadors for Christ, God making his appeal through us. We implore you on behalf of Christ, be reconciled to God.

Christians have an unending life purpose. As long as we have life and breath, we are called to look beyond ourselves to the glory of God and the eternal needs of others. We represent our King Jesus as his ambassadors who proclaim the message of reconciliation to God through him. None of the tinsel of the world can compare to this high calling. We are full-time ambassadors, regardless of our profession or job.

The only reasonable response to the cross of Christ is a life-long offering of yourself to him. Anything less is far too small.

You will have to strive for that. You will need God's help for it; it is impossible to do in your own strength. This life is preparing you for eternity, and that means conforming you to the image of Christ. As God transforms you, he will call and enable you to point others to the cross, thus being Christ's minister of reconciliation to others.

Closing Prayer

My Lord, my God, I am nothing apart from you. But you demonstrated love for me in giving Christ as my Savior; I have great value to you. It is overwhelming to ponder, but also extremely encouraging. Thank you for the great privilege to be adopted into your family, to be made into the likeness of Christ, and to have joy for the present, hope for the future, and assurance that your promises are true. I can believe them without wavering because you are faithful. Help me to live for your glory, the eternal good of other people, and the furtherance of your kingdom. Stir my heart to be your ambassador and minister of reconciliation to our lost and dying world. May I lift high the cross of my Savior, knowing that it is the means by which Jesus draws people to himself. In his mighty name. Amen.

Lifting High the Cross in Worship

Therefore, since we are surrounded by so great a cloud of witnesses, let us also lay aside every weight, and sin which clings so closely, and let us run with endurance the race that is set before us, looking to Jesus, the founder and perfecter of our faith, who for the joy that was set before him endured the cross, despising the shame, and is seated at the right hand of the throne of God. (Hebrews 12:1–2)

THIS FINAL LESSON is devoted to a time of worship, celebrating our crucified, risen Savior. It is based on the lessons from the Scripture and the hymns. Use this for yourself and your group, or prepare your own.

For individuals: Take time to read the Scriptures and hymn texts. Then write your prayers of thanksgiving at each point in the outline. Read each prayer aloud and sing or read aloud each of the hymns. Savor the moments of worship by doing one section each day. Then, review what you have written, praying aloud your prayers and singing or reading aloud the hymns.

For groups: Prior to the group meeting, members should read the Scriptures and hymn texts as well as write the suggested prayers. For the class meeting, members may volunteer to offer their written prayers at the appropriate time in the outline. The group should sing or read together the words of the hymns. Involve as many group members as possible in reading the Scripture passages and offering their prayers. Sing the hymns or read the words. The hymns will become more precious if you study the words and relate them to the lessons on the cross. May you find that the things of earth grow strangely dim as you individually and corporately turn your eyes upon Jesus.

Why We Celebrate

We have cause for celebration as the things of this world have grown and will grow strangely dim in comparison to who Jesus is and what he did.

Hymn: Turn Your Eyes upon Jesus

Before we sing this hymn, note the progression of thought in the verses and chorus.

Why Do We Worship Jesus?

The chorus answers this question.

Turn your eyes upon Jesus,
Look full in His wonderful face;
And the things of earth will grow strangely dim
In the light of his glory and grace.

- We worship Jesus by looking with full attention to his person and by responding with adoration.

- We worship Jesus to see his preeminence over the things of this world.

Who Is Jesus?

Verse 1 tells us who Jesus is.

O soul, are you weary and troubled,
No light in the darkness you see?
There's light for a look at the Savior,
And life more abundant and free.

- Jesus is the only Savior, the giver of abundant and free life, and the light in the darkness.

What Did Jesus Do?

We worship Jesus for what he did for our redemption. Verse 2 tells us what this was.

Through death into life everlasting,
He passed and we follow him there.
Over us sin no more hath dominion,
For more than conquerors we are.

- Jesus passed through death into everlasting life, enabling us to follow him there. We are no longer under the dominion of sin, for in Christ we are more than conquerors, as he is.

Why Can We Trust Jesus?

We worship Jesus because he is trustworthy. Verse 3 tells us why.

His Word shall not fail you, he promised;

Believe him and all will be well.
Then go to a world that is dying,
His perfect salvation to tell.

- We can trust Jesus because his Word is unfailing; his promises are sure. He has given us purpose in life—proclaiming his perfect salvation to a dying world.

Now let us sing this hymn with deeper understanding of Jesus and greater adoration of his person and work.

What Jesus Did

Let us recount what we have learned in this study about what Jesus did.

- He drank the full cup of God's wrath for us in our place. His suffering turned God's anger away from us as he took it on our behalf. We have forgiveness of sin and removal of guilt (1 Peter 2:22–24).

Hymn: Nothing But the Blood of Jesus

The text of this hymn is available in lesson 6.

Prayer

Write a prayer of thanksgiving based on 1 Peter 2:22–24 and the hymn text of "Nothing But the Blood of Jesus."

- He demonstrated his love for us, showing how much he values us (Romans 5:6–8; 1 John 4:9–10).

Our response to his love is to rejoice in it and share it.
Read the words of the song below aloud (individually or as a group) as though you are sharing the truths with other people.

Song: God's Love

Before God made the world, He knew us.
Before God made the world, He loved us.
Before God made the world, He chose us.
We love you, God our Father, because you first loved us.

Oh, who can comprehend God's love for us?
God's love His grace and mercy show.
God's love divine excels all other loves.
God's love, it will not let us go.

Christ came to earth to save us from our sins.
Christ came to earth to show His love for us.
Christ came to earth to give His life for us.
We love you Christ, our Savior, because you first loved us.

Oh, who can comprehend Christ's love for us?
Christ's love redeemed us from our sin.
Christ's love divine excels all other loves.
Christ's love brought us to God again.

O God, your grace has brought us to this day [night].
Your grace will lead us as we seek your way [what's right].
Oh by your grace help us not to stray [keep us in your light].
We love each other, gracious God, because you first loved us.

And now, O God, increase our love for you.
Help us to love each other too.
And now, O God, give us a love for the world.
Teach us to love because you first loved us.

Oh, who can comprehend God's love for us?
God's love, His grace and mercy show.

God's love divine excels all other loves.
God's love, it will not let us go.

—JANE ROACH AND KRISTIN ROACH, © 2000
(For music, see appendix)

Prayer

Write a prayer of thanksgiving based on Ephesians 3:14–21
and the text of "God's Love."

Hymn: Beneath the Cross of Jesus

The text of this hymn is available in lesson 7.

Who Jesus Is

• He lives today as our High Priest and advocate. We are never alone.

▶ READ HEBREWS 2:14–18

▶ READ HEBREWS 7:23–25

Prayer

Write a prayer of adoration and thanksgiving based on the passages from Hebrews.

- He is preeminent over all things and reigns with all authority as God with us.

▶ READ MATTHEW 28:18–20

▶ READ COLOSSIANS 1:15–20

Prayer

Write a prayer of adoration based on the Matthew and Colossians passages.

- He lives in us. We have a new life—his life—by which we run our race for God's glory.

▶ **READ GALATIANS 2:19–20**

Prayer

Write a prayer of thanksgiving based on Galatians 2:19–20.

Prayer

Write a prayer of surrender based on Galatians 2:19–20.

Hymn: "When I Survey the Wondrous Cross"

The text of this hymn is available in lesson 10.

Prayer

Write a prayer of commitment based on the text of "When I Survey the Wondrous Cross."

Now to him who is able to keep you from stumbling and to present you blameless before the presence of his glory with great joy, to the only God, our Savior, through Jesus Christ our Lord, be glory, majesty, dominion, and authority, before all time and now and forever. Amen. (Jude 24–25)

Conclude the time of group worship by reading together Jude 24–25. For individual worship, read the passage aloud.

In light of what we have learned about Jesus' *Joy beyond Agony*, let us embrace the cross in song and proclamation.

Hymn: "Lift High the Cross"[1]

Refrain:
Lift high the cross, the love of Christ proclaim,
till all the world adore his sacred name.

Come, brethren, follow where our Savior trod,
our King victorious, Christ, the Son of God. *Refrain*

Led on their way, by this triumphant sign,
the hosts of God in conqu'ring ranks combine. *Refrain*

O Lord, once lifted on this glorious tree,
as thou hast promised, draw men unto thee. *Refrain*

Thy kingdom come, that earth's despair may cease
beneath the shadow of its healing peace. *Refrain*

For thy blest cross which doth for us atone,
creation's praises rise before thy throne. *Refrain*

1. George W. Kitchin & Michael R. Newbolt © 1974 Hope Publishing Company, Carol Stream, IL 60188. All rights reserved. Used by permission.

God's Love

WHEN MY SON, James Roach, told Jim and me that he wanted to marry Tiffany Cook, we were thrilled. I had learned from experience how love grows in marriage and knew that their love for each other would be tested by life's surprises. As a naval aviator, James would have some deployments away from Tiffany that Jim and I had not experienced. What unknowns would they face in the years ahead, and how would they make it through them?

I began to pray for them to be assured of God's great love for them, expressed in the sacrificial death of his Son Jesus Christ on their behalf, and that they would love each other because he first loved them. With God's love as their focus, I knew he would teach them how to love each other and then how to love those beyond their own home and family—even those around the world. As I prayed, God put the words to this song in my mind and the simple tune followed. My daughter, Kristin Roach, added the finishing touch with her beautiful arrangement. It was our gift to James and Tiffany that was sung at their rehearsal dinner on September 8, 2000. God has abundantly answered my prayers for them. After almost fifteen years of marriage and four children, their love for the God who first loved them has grown. They have sacrificially loved each other through some difficult times, and they extend kindness and grace to people beyond their own home. To God be the glory!

God's Love

For James and Tiffany Roach

Words and Melody by Jane Roach
Arranged by Kristin Roach

287

who can com-pre-hend Christ's love for us? Christ's love re-deemed us from our sin. Christ's

who can com-pre-hend Christ's love for us? Christ's love re-deemed us from our sin. Christ's

love di-vine ex-cels all oth-er loves. Christ's love brought us to God a-gain.

love di-vine ex-cels all oth-er loves. Christ's love brought us to God a-gain.

289

291

Recommended Reading

Bennett, Arthur. *The Valley of Vision: A Collection of Puritan Prayers & Devotions.* Carlisle, PA: Banner of Truth, 1988.

Boice, James Montgomery, and Philip Graham Ryken. *The Heart of the Cross.* Wheaton, IL: Crossway, 1999.

Elliot, Elisabeth. *Discipline: The Glad Surrender.* 1982. Reprint, Grand Rapids, MI: Revell, 2006.

Fitzpatrick, Elyse M., and Dennis E. Johnson. *Counsel from the Cross: Connecting Broken People to the Love of Christ.* Wheaton, IL: Crossway, 2009.

Foxe, John. *Foxe's Book of Martyrs.* John Day, 1563. Reprint, Peabody, MA: Hendrickson Publishers, 2004.

Guthrie, Nancy, ed. *Jesus, Keep Me Near the Cross: Experiencing the Passion and Power of Easter.* Wheaton, IL: Crossway, 2009.

Schreiner, Thomas R. *Romans.* Baker Exegetical Commentary on the New Testament. Grand Rapids, MI: Baker Academic, 1998.

Sproul, R.C. *Saved from What?* Wheaton, IL: Crossway, 2002.

Thomas, Derek W. H. *How the Gospel Brings Us All the Way Home.* Orlando, FL: Reformation Trust, 2011.

Tozer, A. W. *The Pursuit of God.* Camp Hill, PA: Christian Publications, 1982.